The Answer Book

Small-Group Guide

Worldview Series

NANCY RUTH

WESTBOW®
PRESS
A DIVISION OF THOMAS NELSON
& ZONDERVAN

THE HOLY BIBLE, NEW INTERNATIONAL VERSION®, NIV® Copyright © 1973, 1978, 1984, 2011 by Biblica, Inc.® Used by permission. All rights reserved worldwide. Scripture taken from the NEW AMERICAN STANDARD BIBLE®, Copyright ©1960, 1962, 1963, 1968, 1971, 1972, 1973, 1975, 1977, 1995 by The Lockman Foundation. Used by permission. Scripture taken from *The Message.* Copyright ©1993, 1994, 1995, 1996, 2000, 2001, 2002. Used by permission of NavPress Publishing Group. Scripture taken from *Easy-to-Read Version,* Copyright ©2006 World Bible Translation Center.

WestBow Press books may be ordered through booksellers or by contacting:

WestBow Press
A Division of Thomas Nelson & Zondervan
1663 Liberty Drive
Bloomington, IN 47403
www.westbowpress.com
1 (866) 928-1240

ISBN: 978-1-4908-6888-2 (sc)
ISBN: 978-1-4908-6889-9 (e)

Library of Congress Control Number: 2015901803

Printed in the United States of America.

WestBow Press rev. date: 2/10/2015

Contents

Why Are There Two Guides?

The partnering study, *The Answer Book: A Devotional for Busy Families,* is written to do at home as individual family groups. There are several ways you can come together to share, encourage each other, and continue to grow in this study.

You may choose to keep your families together and meet as a multigenerational group. If so, follow the "Guide for Multigenerational and Children's Groups."

You may choose to split up to dig deeper on age-appropriate levels. If so, children's groups should follow the "Guide for Multigenerational and Children's Groups." Adults should follow the "Guide for Adult Groups." Teenagers may either join the adults or co-teach the children. Group leaders may also pull from the first and/or second guides to craft their own lessons.

You do not need to be a seasoned small-group leader to use either of these guides. Here is the test.

- Do you love the Lord?
- Do you love people? (It can be in a quiet way or in an extroverted way.)
- Are you not perfect?
- Are you and your family using (or planning to use) *The Answer Book: A Devotional for Busy Families*?
- Can you commit to being at the small-group meeting every week (or securing a substitute) for the next seven weeks?

If you answered yes to all these questions, you can lead this study. Everything is written out for you. It is better if you can study it in advance, but in a pinch, you can read it right off the page. You are even warned of any supplies.

Each guide includes a brief overview page, a more in-depth "How Does This Work?", teaching tips (including how to get a discussion going in a quiet group), a guide on how to lead a person to Christ, and suggestions for how to combine two lessons into one. Lessons are broken into parts to be easily adaptable for each group's needs. Every lesson includes Bible reading, discussion, application, and prayer, though the proportions vary.

May God bless you as you prepare to dig into His Word together.

Nancy Ruth
Parent Road Ministries

Part 1

Guide for Multigenerational or Children's Groups

- Opening Activities (optional): Bible skills, introductory activity, and/or music
- Bible Focus (optional★): A short Bible lesson
- Application Activities: Family challenge review, craft, and/or game
- Wrap It Up: Review that week's main point
- Prayer Time: Take prayer requests and close with a prayer focus

The "Guide for Adult Groups" begins on page 73.

★If not also using *The Answer Book: A Devotional for Busy Families*, please include the Bible Focus.

How Does This Work?

This small-group guide is designed for groups of two or more children or families. It could be used for a group of friends meeting regularly, breakfast groups, Bible study groups, Sunday school, a weekend family retreat, or any number of other occasions.

This guide has two sections, broken down to allow leaders to choose what works best within time constraints. This section includes the "Guide for Multigenerational and Children's Groups." The "Guide for Adult Groups" begins on page 73.

Younger children are those in second grade or lower. Older children are in third grade or higher. The Main Idea of each lesson is adapted to be memorable for these two age groups.

Leaders are encouraged to choose at least one Application Activity, Wrap It Up, and use the Prayer Focus The rest is optional, depending on your time and format. Little to zero leader prep time is required for all activities.

- *Opening Activities* (optional)—Choose at least one of the following: Bible Skills, Introductory Activity, and/or Music.
- *Bible Focus* (optional*)—Engage learners to participate in the Bible lesson.
- *Application Activities*—Choose at least one of the following to apply the lesson of the week: family challenge review (from the *Devotional for Busy Families*), Craft, and/or Game. The "On the Road Family Challenge" is found in *The Answer Book: A Devotional for Busy Families*. These challenges may also be used apart from this devotional.
- *Wrap It Up*—Bring the focus back at the close of the lesson to briefly review that week's main point.
- *Prayer Focus*—Take prayer requests, and close with a prayer linking back to that day's lesson.

    *This study is designed to partner with *The Answer Book: A Devotional for Busy Families*, but it may also stand alone. If not partnering with the *Devotional for Busy Families*, be sure to include the Bible Focus. If you are using the *Devotional for Busy Families*, do the first week of the separate daily Bible study, gather your group, and then start with Week 1 in this guide.

Group members do not need to bring anything, though some may like to bring their Bibles.

Each week please be sure to include the following in your study.

- Encourage group members to *read the Bible* daily. This is not meant to be a guilt trip. When a day or more is missed, just pick up where you left off and keep going.
- Encourage group members to *apply* what they are learning with their families.
- *Pray together.* We cannot do any of this trusting in only our strength.

If your situation allows, I encourage you to keep an open door policy, welcoming new people at any time. This would apply even to those who might miss a week or two (or more).

Find a regular time for your group to meet, and let's get started!

Teaching Tips

- *Provide a safe place.* Be sure to emphasize to your group members that what is said there should stay there. Without that kind of setting, you will not be able to build the trust and genuine sharing that fosters accountability and greatly aids spiritual growth.

- *Elevate the Prayer Focus.* If your group runs long, it is recommended that either the Prayer Focus opens your time together or the discussion be cut short to allow time for prayer at the end.

- *Feel free to change the order.* As the leader, you have freedom to arrange your class time to make it work best. Choose the activities you think will best present the lesson, and arrange them in the order to best suit. Keep in mind that different people learn in different ways, so try to provide a variety of activities over the next few weeks. They don't all have to be in the same lesson.

- *If you cancel a small-group meeting for any reason, do not cancel the at-home daily Bible study.* Strive to make Bible study a daily habit, no matter what life throws at you (see Psalm 1:1–3). See page 10 for suggestions on how to combine two weeks into one for the gathering following your canceled meeting.

- *Stay positive.* Changing habits is hard. Encourage progress wherever you see it, no matter how small. This is especially important with children. They do not control everything in their lives (like whether they have a family Bible study). Encourage them to read the Bible, to pray, and to love God and other people. Just like God meets us where we are, loves us, and takes us from there, so we do with other people as His followers.

- *Let people talk.* People feel valued when they are allowed to say what they have to say. This also fosters discussion. When people feel like they are cut off, they may begin to stop talking all together (unless they simply love to talk).

- *Avoid monopolies.* Do the same few people in your group answer all the questions and everyone else just sits there? Try naming a name before you ask a question. Allow the person time to think, but if he or she truly doesn't know, ask if the individual would like some help. Then either let the person choose a friend, or you can ask someone else. Make a point to draw out the quiet ones. You may be surprised what they contribute. Keep in mind that introverts often find it easier to begin by sharing ideas about things outside of themselves or about other (even hypothetical) people. Sharing their deeper thoughts, feelings, and personal stories, especially ones that involve hurt or shame, is a sign of great trust. It is not usually given lightly.

- *Don't be afraid of the silence.* Some groups take longer than others to respond to discussion questions, and that's okay. If you provide the answer too soon, you may be fostering a spirit of "wait for the teacher to provide the right answer." Try instead something like, "This is the discussion part," or ask if you need to repeat the question. You might also try going around the room for everyone to answer until your group gets the hang of discussion. But be aware some may be uncomfortable speaking in that setting.

- *Ask more questions.* Is your group reluctant to talk? While avoiding keeping the spotlight on anyone too long, ask follow-up questions to the short answers you get. Think of the 5 Ws and 1 H: In a show of hands, *who* else feels this way? *Who* else has experienced _____ (follow up on what was said or refer back to the original question)? *What* might that look like? Can you describe a time in your life *when* God reminded you of that very thing? *What* might be a situation *where* we might need to remember that? *Where* might we need to remember this? (After you get an answer to that question follow it with, *Why* that place? Then go back to the first and go again.) *Why* is this important? *How* do you know? What other questions can you think of? If you have trouble thinking of questions on the spot, make a list and keep it with your book.

- *If you have time, prepare Scriptures in advance.* Write or print the Bible references you will be using (or the whole verse) on separate slips of paper. As group members come, ask if they would be willing to read a verse. If so, give them one or more of your papers, have them look them up, and bookmark them to have them ready to read when needed. Be sure to provide extra Bibles. Keep in mind this takes longer if children are reading.

- *When choosing a version of Scripture to use as a "teaching Bible," consider your audience.* I usually recommend the *New International Version* (NIV) or *English Standard Version* (ESV) for children, but you may choose whichever version you like. Keep in mind that King James may require much more explanation on your part, since children are not as familiar with that form of English. One way to think of the different versions of the Bible is like the accelerated reader (AR) levels children are so familiar with from school. Children use the AR levels to choose books based on their reading ability. The higher the AR level, the harder the book. Different translations of the Bible serve a similar purpose. The original text was written in Greek, Hebrew, and Aramaic. These languages are very different from English in the way words and phrases are put together, not to mention what words mean. Some words have no exact word-to-word correlation. This makes it challenging to translate. For example, some of Paul's original Greek sentences, while grammatically correct for his day and language, would horrify English teachers today. His run-on sentences seem to last forever! Some English translations (like the *New American Standard Bible*) stay as close as they can to the original text and may seem harder to understand. Other English versions (like *The Message*) decide to take the meaning of the text and put it into easy to understand modern speech. Others (like the NIV) try to stay in the middle of the two extremes. The ESV is slightly easier to understand than the NIV.

- *Don't have a Bible?* Several good Bible apps are available, like the *YouBible*. You can also look up verses at www.biblegateway.com. Just type the reference as you see it into the search box. Be sure to scroll all the way down the page in case the verses appear in more than one frame. Many children may associate phones and the Internet primarily with games. It may be best to use a physical Bible with this age group.

- *New to using the Bible?* No problem! Scripture verses are given as book chapter:verse (i.e., Luke 3:2). Look up the book in the table of contents. Once you are in the right book, chapters are designated with either large numbers or headings, like "Chapter 1." Under each chapter number come smaller verse numbers, which restart with each chapter. Sometimes chapters continue into the next column or page. Deuteronomy 6:4–6, for example, would be the book of Deuteronomy (the fifth book of the Bible), the large number 6 (or the heading "Chapter 6"), and the smaller numbers 4, 5, and 6 within that chapter. Hint 1: Usually verse 1 is not numbered. Hint 2: Verses continue all the way until the next number, for example, "⁴Hear, O Israel: The Lord our God, the Lord is one. ⁵Love the Lord your God with all your heart and with all your soul and with all your strength. ⁶These commandments that I give you today are to be on your hearts."

How to Lead a Person to Christ

1) The first step is to *admit* (agree with God) *that you are a sinner.*

All we have to offer God that He[1] wants is our hearts broken over our sins. Tell Him you are sorry, and turn from your sins. Try not to do them anymore through God's forgiveness, mercy, and strength.

> Repent, then, and turn to God, so that your sins may be wiped out, that times of refreshing may come from the Lord, and that he may send the Messiah, who has been appointed for you—even Jesus. (Acts 3:19–20 NIV)

> The sacrifices of God are a broken spirit; A broken and a contrite heart, O God, You[2] will not despise. (Psalm 51:17 NASB; see also Ephesians 2:8–9; Isaiah 64:6)

A person ready to accept Christ as his or her Lord and Savior should understand the disconnect between God's perfect holiness and our sinful imperfections. Ask the following questions.

- What is heaven like? (See Revelation 21:1–22:7; Isaiah 11; 65:17–25.)
- Who lives in heaven? (See Acts 7:55–56; Isaiah 6:1–7; Revelation 4–5; 6:9–11; 7:4–17.)
- What is sin? (The wrong stuff we do: any thought, word, deed, or thing left undone that does not meet God's perfect standard. See Leviticus 11:45.)
- Can you name some sins? (See, for example, Romans 1:28–32.)
- Have you ever sinned? (Romans 3:23. God's perfection is the standard—Matthew 5:48; Leviticus 11:44.)

2) The second step is to *believe that Jesus is God's Son and that He died and rose again to pay for your sins.* Basically, Jesus is who He says He is, and He died and rose again to pay for our sins (1 Corinthians 15:3–4).

> that if you confess with your mouth Jesus as Lord, and believe in your heart that God raised Him from the dead, you will be saved; for with the heart a person believes, resulting in righteousness, and with the mouth he confesses, resulting in salvation. (Romans 10:9–10 NASB; see also 2 Corinthians 5:17)

A person ready to accept Christ as his or her Lord and Savior should understand who Jesus is and believe in Him. Ask the following questions.

- Who is Jesus? What did He do?
- Did Jesus ever sin? (Not even once! See Hebrews 4:15; 2 Corinthians 5:21.)
- Why did Jesus die on the cross? Did He stay dead? (See 1 Corinthians 15:3–7.)
- Where is Jesus now? (Jesus is alive and seated at the right hand of God the Father in heaven. See Acts 1:9–11; 2:32–34. The Holy Spirit lives in the hearts of those who trust Him as their Lord and Savior. See John 14:16–18.)
- How can our sins be forgiven? (See Romans 10:9–10; John 1:12; 3:16.)
- What does "Savior" mean?
- Do you believe Jesus is who He says He is and that He did all of these things? (See Romans 10:9–10.)

3) The third step is to *commit to Jesus as your Lord and Savior.*

"Commit" means to decide to do something—decide firmly where nothing will change your mind. There will be times when this is difficult and times when it seems impossible, but God will help you (John 10:28–30; 1 Corinthians 10:13).

As Savior, Jesus took our penalty (punishment) for sin (Romans 5:8). Jesus takes our punishment, so our sins are forgiven and wiped clean forever (Psalm 103:12; Isaiah 1:18; 1 John 1:9; 1 Peter 3:18).

As Lord, Jesus is our life leader and worthy of our utmost respect and worship (Ephesians 1:20–22; Philippians 2:6–11).

A person ready to accept Christ as their Lord and Savior should understand this is a *lifetime commitment.* Ask the following questions.

- What does it meant to commit your life to Christ? (See Luke 9:23.)
- What does "Lord" mean?
- After we ask Jesus to be our Savior, will we ever sin again? (See Romans 7:18–20; 1 Corinthians 10:13.)
- What happens then? What do we do? (Turn from your sin, ask for forgiveness, and try not to do it again. God will help you; 1 Corinthians 10:13.)
- Are you ready to make this lifelong commitment to follow Jesus Christ as Lord and Savior, no matter what?

Let them pray and then pray for them, asking God to continue to teach them more about Him and draw them closer to Him.

How to Combine Two Weeks into One

There are several reasons small group may be canceled (holidays, weather emergencies, etc.). Here are some tips on how to adapt this curriculum in those situations.

1. Encourage the parents and members of your small group to continue with their daily Bible study, *even when you are not meeting*. Our relationship with God does not stop when we go on vacation. It does take conscious thought—and sometimes effort—to continue to make time with Him part of our day.

    If the members of your group don't actually finish every day while on vacation, that's fine. Celebrate the days you *did* do and keep going on together.

    > Blessed is the one
    > … whose delight is in the law of the LORD,[3]
    >   and who meditates on his law day and night.
    > That person is like a tree planted by streams of water,
    >   which yields its fruit in season
    > and whose leaf does not wither—
    >   whatever they do prospers. (Psalm 1:1–3 NIV)

    Studies have shown that people will perform automated behaviors—like pulling out of a driveway or brushing teeth—the same way every single time, if they're in the same environment. But if they take a vacation, it's likely that the behavior will change.[4]

2. In the meeting following your break,

*   Choose which of the two weeks you would like to do as a group, and skip the other.

    ◦   For example,
        Last time you met you did Week 3.
        You did Week 4 in the at-home daily Bible study.
        When you meet again, you will discuss Week 5 as a small group.

*   If you are able to continue meeting after the at-home study ends, go back and do the missed week. Review never hurts.

Week 1: What Is A Worldview?

"Cows don't intend to get lost," the farmer explained,
"they just nibble their way to lostness!"[5]
… None of us intends to wander from the green pasture of God's voice!
None of us intends to have our souls wander onto the dull
and listless highway of the American Way.
First comes the tuft of education, then the tuft of marriage, then children, a new home,
and one day we wake up to discover that we have nibbled our way to lostness."

Michael Yaconelli[6]

Main Point (Say this a lot today.)

Younger Kids: God's Word says what is good and bad.
Older Kids: God's Word is the standard for what is right or wrong.

Scripture

The wise man built his house upon the rock. (Matthew 7:24–29)

Prepare Your Heart to Teach

When you have to make a tough decision, where is the first place you go for advice?

The Lord says in Jeremiah 33:3 (NIV), "Call to me and I will answer you and tell you great and unsearchable things you do not know."

God's Word is the standard of truth, because God is all things good, noble, right, and true. "As for God, his way is perfect: The Lord's word is flawless; he shields all who take refuge in him" (Psalm 18:30 NIV).

Do you trust God enough to take Him at His Word? Do you trust Him with your life? All of it?

Week 1: Opening Activities (optional)

Do at least one of the following activities.

That Book!

Younger Kids: God's Word says what is good and bad.
Older Kids: God's Word is the standard for what is right or wrong.

Feel free to find more ideas at *www.MrMarksClassroom.com.*

Supplies Needed: Bibles; signs saying "Matthew," "Mark," "Luke," "John" (optional)

Advanced Preparation (optional): Hang the signs in the four corners of the room.

Name each corner of the room for one of the Gospels. When the leader calls out one of these books, everyone runs to that corner. If you hear "Genesis," stop where you are, and lie on the floor or touch your knees. When you hear "Revelation," wave your hands in the air and shout, "Halleluiah!"

Ready? Set ... John! Call out various books. After playing for a while, gather the troops to discuss. You may play again at the end if you have time.

God's Word is the standard for what is right or wrong, so it is important to know your way around it. Genesis is the first book of the Bible. (Practice finding it.) Genesis 1–3 tell how the world began. Revelation is the last book of the Bible. (Practice finding it.) Revelation tells about when Jesus will come back from heaven. His people will join the angels worshipping Him and say, "Halleluiah!" (Revelation 5; 7:4–17; 19; 22). The first four books of the New Testament tell us the most about Jesus. They are Matthew, Mark, Luke, and John. Together they are called the Gospels. To find the Gospels, open your Bible in the very middle. You should be in or near Psalms. Now open the right half of the Bible in the middle. Since there are four Gospels, let's name them four times together. (Hold up your fingers to count how many times you say them.) Matthew, Mark, Luke, John, Matthew ... You should be in or near the Gospels. (Practice together.) What is the first book of the Bible? What is the last book of the Bible? What are the four Gospels?

Two Houses

Younger Kids: God's Word says what is good and bad.
Older Kids: God's Word is the standard for what is right or wrong.

Supplies Needed: A large pillow or not-so-neatly-folded blanket and blocks or other stackable, non-linking building materials (Hint: Legos, KNEX, and so on may not work well for this activity.)

Divide the group in half, providing each with building materials. Challenge them to build a house in the time allotted, one on the solid floor and one on the pillow or blanket.

Which surface was easier to build on—the floor or the blanket/pillow? Why?

What do you think might happen if someone jumped right next to your house—not *on* it but on the floor *next* to it? Try it—first one person and then the whole group.

Which house lasted longer when the earthquake hit?

In today's Bible lesson, we will hear Jesus tell about houses built on sand and rock. He won't really be talking about houses. He's really talking about what happens when we make decisions. We can choose to make decisions based on what God's Word says or not. God's Word tells us what is true. Listen carefully, and see if you can tell which house is a picture of making good decisions based on the truth of God's Word.

Music

Younger Kids: God's Word says what is good and bad.
Older Kids: God's Word is the standard for what is right or wrong.

Supplies Needed: A willingness to worship God through singing (Did I say sing well? Children just need someone to lead them. They are not critics.), CD and player (optional), computer with speakers (optional), DVD and player (optional), phone with music player (optional), instrument with player and music (optional)

Advanced Preparation: Choose the songs and how you will lead them.

Following you will find a variety of songs and styles. Please do not try to do them all. If you choose to do music, I recommend learning three to four songs over the course of the next seven weeks. Choose what works best for your group. For children, I would choose mostly fast songs and end with one slower, worshipful song. You decide what that means for your group. Feel free to change the order of the categories listed below. These songs may be found on *YouTube* and may be purchased on *iTunes* or CD. Some are also available on DVD.

God's Word Is the Source of Truth

"Jesus Loves Me" (There are lots of variations of this, for example, "Hey! Jesus Loves Me!" "Jesus Loves Me Rock")

There are several books of the Bible songs and raps. One puts the books to the tune of "Ten Little Indians."

"The Wise Man and the Foolish Man" ("The wise man built his house upon the rock …")

"Wonderful Words of Life," by Philip P. Bliss

Who God Is

"Better Is One Day," by Matt Redman or Kutless

"My God Is so Big"

"One Way," by Hillsong Kids

"Tell Me the Stories of Jesus," by Parker and Challinor

God Loves Me

"Amazing Grace" (or "My Chains Are Gone," by Chris Tomlin)

"He Knows My Name," by Maranatha Singers

"Get Down," by Audio Adrenaline

"Supernatural," by Hillsong Kids

Week 1: Bible Focus (optional[7])

Younger Kids: God's Word says what is good and bad.
Older Kids: God's Word is the standard for what is right or wrong.

Supplies Needed: Bible to teach from, paper, pencils or markers/crayons

Challenge listeners to draw what they hear. They may also choose to write down any questions they have or words that sound important as you speak. At the end, ask for questions, and allow at least a few to share their pictures and what they learned.

People knew Jesus was different from the other teachers. Jesus explained God's Word better than anyone else, because He is God. He helped the Old Testament writers know what to say, so He knew exactly what God meant by the words they wrote (John 1:1–5, 14–15).[8] This amazed people, and they would gather in huge crowds to hear Jesus teach.

One day when a big crowd came to listen, Jesus taught them many things. Then He told them this story to remind them to always do what God's Word says.

Read Matthew 7:24–29. Don't forget to add plenty of expression.

Do you think it's a good idea to build your house on a rock? Why or why not?

If you build your house on a rock and a big storm comes, like a hurricane or tornado, what happens?

Do you think it's a good idea to build your house on the sand? Why or why not?

Storms are hard on houses. What hard things can happen to us? (Start with an example from your life, like getting really sick, losing someone close to you, friends being really mean to you, etc. Be sure to include how that made you feel.)

What do you think Jesus meant when He said that if we listen to and obey God's Word, we are like a man who builds his house on the rock?

Psalm 95:1 (NIV) says, "Come, let us sing for joy to the Lord; let us shout aloud to the Rock of our salvation." God shows us in His Word how He is always with us. He also shows us how we can weather the storms of life, the bad things that happen to us, by trusting in Him. God comforts us and gives us the strength we lack. Most of all, Jesus provided the way for us to be saved from our sins. God is so good! All we need to do is turn to Him and trust Him. Do you?

When we build our lives and trust in other things, we might survive smaller storms, but when the big one hits, everything we thought was important will fall apart. Only a life built on Jesus Christ will stand the test of time and be able to weather all life's storms (John 3:36).

Remember that God is always with you, no matter what. Hebrews 13:5 says, "Never will I leave you; never will I forsake you." (See also Joshua 1:5; Psalm 129:7–12).

If You Have Time: Ask for questions, and allow at least a few to share their pictures and one thing they learned.

Week 1: Application Activities

Do at least one of the following activities.

On the Road Family Challenge Review[9]

Younger Kids: God's Word says what is good and bad.
Older Kids: God's Word is the standard for what is right or wrong.

Supplies Needed: Paper, pencils, markers/crayons

Your mission is for everyone to make a list (or pictures) of things they see that are different from what God's Word (the Bible) teaches. If you have very young kids, be sure to include them. They may surprise you. Lists don't have to be perfect. Everyone should just do their best. Share your lists, and talk about how God's Word tells us what is right or wrong and what we should do.

Questions for each person:

What did you find that is different from what God's Word says? (Or, for young children, what did someone do today that was a bad choice?)

What does God's Word say about this? (Alternately, what would be a better choice?)

God's Word is the standard for what is right or wrong.

Worldview Collage

Younger Kids: God's Word says what is good and bad.
Older Kids: God's Word is the standard for what is right or wrong.

Supplies Needed: Paper, poster board, or large paper; markers; scissors (optional); glue (optional); magazines or pictures (optional)

The following is adapted from Day 1 of *The Answer Book: A Devotional for Busy Families* (used by permission).

What is your favorite food? What kind of clothes do you like? Who is in your family? What is one thing you do at work or school ("homemaker" counts as work)? What is your favorite movie or actor? What games do you like? What is your favorite song or type of music? What is one thing you do every week? What do you like to do at church? Who is your best friend?

All these things shape what is called a "worldview." Say that together: "worldview." Does anyone in your family wear glasses? When someone sees things around them as fuzzy or blurry, he or she gets glasses, which helps the person see more clearly. Just like glasses, a worldview helps us see the world more clearly and make decisions more easily. It helps us decide what is good to eat, what to wear, what to do with our time, how to treat other people, and how to think about things. We learn how to do this from our family, friends, teachers, churches, and other things we see and hear, like TV, music, books, games, and movies.

God's Word answers questions about how to treat others, how to use our time, and how to think about things. Often, the answers God's Word provides will be different from what some music, movies, games, and people around us say. Remember that God always knows best. His Word, the Bible, is the standard for what is right or wrong.

Make a worldview collage. Cut out or draw pictures of different things that are part of a worldview. You may make one big poster or have each family make its own.

God's Word Says …

Younger Kids: God's Word says what is good and bad.
Older Kids: God's Word is the standard for what is right or wrong.

Supplies Needed: None

God's Word is the standard for what is right or wrong. We're going to play a game to help us see how this works.

This game is played like "Simon Says." Name several activities that God's Word either says to do or doesn't say to do. If you say "God's Word says …" then everyone should pretend to do it. If not, they can either stand still or wag their finger and say something like, "God's Word didn't say."

Here are a few to get you started.

- God's Word says to obey your mom when she tells you to pick up your toys.
- God's Word says to talk to God in prayer.
- Take the remote away from your sister.
- God's Word says to love your friend by giving high fives.
- Be mean to your friend.
- God's Word says to use kind words like "please" and "thank you."
- Lie to your friends.
- God's Word says to worship God by singing.
- God's Word says to go to church.

- Hit your brother.
- God's Word says to be nice to others, like sitting by the new kid at school.

Week 1: Wrap It Up

Younger Kids: God's Word says what is good and bad.
Older Kids: God's Word is the standard for what is right or wrong.

All Scripture is God-breathed and is useful for teaching, rebuking, correcting and training in righteousness, so that the servant of God may be thoroughly equipped for every good work. (2 Timothy 3:16–17 NIV)

All we need to know about right from wrong and how to live life can be found in God's Word. That is why it is important to read it, study it, and do what it says.

Isn't God good to give us everything we need in His Word?

Week 1: Prayer Focus

Younger Kids: God's Word says what is good and bad.
Older Kids: God's Word is the standard for what is right or wrong.

Doom to you! You pretend to have the inside track.
    You shut God out and work behind the scenes,
Plotting the future as if you knew everything,
    acting mysterious, never showing your hand.
You have everything backward!
    You treat the potter as a lump of clay.
Does a book say to its author,
    "He didn't write a word of me"?
Does a meal say to the woman who cooked it,
    "She had nothing to do with this"? (Isaiah 29:15–16 MSG)

God's plan is not a secret. He wants us to seek and follow Him. He has promised to give us everything we need, for He knows those things better than we do. Are there any special prayer requests this week?

End your prayer time asking God to show you what His Word says and how to know right from wrong (good choices from bad choices).

Week 2: Is There Only One Truth?

Only Scripture can claim to have absolute truth, for only it comes straight to us from God Himself. Knowledge that we gain from the use of the scientific method still comes to us through people ... People are flawed, and, therefore, the results of their efforts, no matter how careful and sincere they may be, are also flawed. This is why so many scientific studies, even in the realm of the natural or "hard" sciences are later contradicted by other studies.

John Babler, David Penley, and Mike Bizzell[10]

Main Point (Say this a lot today.)

Younger and Older Kids: God's Word tells us what is true.

Scripture

Elijah and the prophets of Baal (pronounced "bah-AHL" or Anglicized "BAIL") (1 Kings 18:17–40).

Prepare Your Heart to Teach

Jesus answered, "I am the way and the truth and the life. No one comes to the Father except through me." (John 14:6 NIV)

Do you believe Jesus is the only way to a full and eternal life? Here's the challenge: if you do, do you live that way?

The thief comes only to steal and kill and destroy; I have come that they may have life, and have it to the full. (John 10:10 NIV)

It is easy to get distracted, sidetracked, and even deceived from what God tells us is true. When we keep our eyes fixed on Jesus, the truth sets us free. We can live every day in that freedom.

So if the Son sets you free, you will be free indeed. (John 8:36 NIV)

The trick is to meditate on the truth, Jesus Christ, who's coming, life, and work is recorded for us in the Bible.

Week 2: Opening Activity (optional)

Do at least one of the following activities.

What Is True? What Is Not?

Younger and Older Kids: God's Word tells us what is true.

Feel free to repeat previous Bible activities or find more ideas at *www.MrMarksClassroom.com.*

Supplies Needed: Bibles, individual cards for the books; today we're using Genesis to Esther (see *www.sundayschoolsources.com/books-bible-bingo.htm* for premade cards), list or poster of all the Bible books (optional)

Advanced Preparation (optional): Lay out the Bible book cards in order on the floor.

God's Word tells us what is true. When we study what is true, we can more easily spot what is not. Draw attention to your Bible book cards. Say the names of the books Genesis to Esther in order together. Have the group turn to look at the wall opposite the cards, so they can't peek. Change a few cards. For a younger group, turn a card sideways, face down, or with the text upside down. For an older group, switch cards or take away one or more. Have the group face the cards again and ask, "What is true? What is not?" When a change has been found, ask, "What is true? What should really be there?" Once the changes have been found and fixed, say the names of all the books and play again.

Challenge: Ask one or two group members to leave the room while the rest of the group changes a few cards. Absent members then return and try to find what is true and what is not.

After playing for a while, gather the troops to practice finding Genesis, Revelation, Psalms, and the Gospels. (See Week 1.) You may play again at the end if you have time.

Sorting Race

Younger and Older Kids: God's Word tells us what is true.

Supplies Needed: A timer, two pairs of things to sort (e.g., crayons vs. markers; living vs. not; paper vs. other; books vs. Bibles; toys vs. tools; round vs. angles, etc.)

This is a beat the clock game. Pile one pair of items (e.g., crayons vs. markers) together in one mixed pile across the room from the participants. (Save the second paring for round 2.) If you do not have a starting line marked on the floor, it works well for participants (especially kids) to have to touch the wall before you say, "Go." When you say, "Go," participants must hurry to the pile of items and work together to sort them into two piles.

For a younger group, provide the two sorting categories.

For an older group, challenge them to find their own sorting categories, but limit it to two piles.

Once they have completed the challenge, all participants must be back at the starting line to stop the clock.

Before the second race, discuss. Was it hard or easy to sort the pile? Why? Is it hard or easy to know what is right or wrong? How can we know for sure what is right or wrong? Let the group answer before you give today's focus: God's Word is the standard for what is right or wrong. Sometimes we have to work to find the answers to our questions in God's Word, but He promises to give us wisdom if we ask for it (James 1:5). Wisdom is understanding and doing what God asks us to do. As I get ready, ask God to help you understand and know the difference between right and wrong.

Collect the items, and put down the second mixed pairing. Challenge the group to beat their time sorting items as a team.

Music

Younger and Older Kids: God's Word tells us what is true.

Supplies Needed: A willingness to worship God through singing (Did I say sing "well"? Children just need someone to lead them. They are not critics.), CD and player (optional), computer with speakers (optional), DVD and player (optional), phone with music player (optional), instrument with player and music (optional)

Advanced Preparation: Choose the songs and how you will lead them.

Following you will find a variety of songs and styles. Please do not try to do them all. If you choose to do music, I recommend learning three to four songs over the course of the next seven weeks. You choose what works best for your group. For children, I would choose mostly fast songs and end with one slower, worshipful song. You decide what that means for your group. Feel free to change the order of the categories. All these songs may be found on *YouTube* and may be purchased on iTunes or CD. Some are also available on DVD.

God's Word Is the Source of Truth

"Jesus Loves Me" (There are lots of variations of this, e.g., "Hey! Jesus Loves Me!" "Jesus Loves Me Rock")

There are several books of the Bible songs and raps. One puts the books to the tune of "Ten Little Indians."

"The Wise Man and the Foolish Man" ("The wise man built his house upon the rock …")

"Wonderful Words of Life," by Philip P. Bliss

Who God Is

"Better Is One Day," by Matt Redman or Kutless

"My God Is so Big"

"One Way," by Hillsong Kids

"Tell Me the Stories of Jesus," by Parker and Challinor

God Loves Me

"Amazing Grace" (or "My Chains Are Gone," by Chris Tomlin)

"He Knows My Name," by Maranatha Singers

"Get Down," by Audio Adrenaline

"Supernatural," by Hillsong Kids

Week 2: Bible Focus (optional[7])

Younger and Older Kids: God's Word tells us what is true.

Supplies Needed: Two chairs (if acting out the story and not using people to be altars)

Learners may either act out the story as you tell it or show with their faces what the crowd might have been thinking at certain places in the story. If you choose to act out the story, assign the following roles. Characters in bold work well for groups of people Roles in parenthesis are optional.

Elijah
Prophets of Baal (pronounced "bah-AHL" or Anglicized "BAIL")
(1–4 water carriers)
(King Ahab)
(watching crowd)
(1–2 Altars): When you are "built," go up on your hands and knees like a horse or sit in a chair.

(fire): Crouch down around Elijah's altar, and spring to life
   (stand up, waving your hands in the air) when needed.
(prophets of Asherah) (pronounced "ASH-uh-ruh")

Elijah was a man who loved God. He lived at a time when the people of Israel were not following God. They knew who God was, but they chose to listen to King Ahab and Queen Jezebel, who told them Baal and Asherah were the real gods, and they should worship them. Were King Ahab and Queen Jezebel right? Let's see what happened.

Read 1 Kings 18:18–21. (Show on your face what you might have been thinking if you were in the crowd.)

Then Elijah presented the challenge. It would be Elijah and God Almighty versus the 450 prophets of Baal and their god. Each team would build their own altar and cut up meat to sacrifice to their god on it. The catch was that they could not set the fire.

Read 1 Kings 18:24. (Show on your face what you might have been thinking if you were in the crowd.)

Elijah gave the other side every home team advantage. He gave them first choice on which meat to sacrifice (1 Kings 18:23). He even let them go first that morning and stayed quiet for several hours to let them do what they wished.

Read 1 Kings 18:26. (Show on your face what you might have been thinking if you were in the crowd.)

Read 1 Kings 18:27–29. (Caution: In verse 28, the priests cut themselves to try to draw the attention of their god. You may choose to edit this for very young children, move very quickly over these verses, or prepare for any questions that may arise.[11]) (Show on your face what you might have been thinking if you were in the crowd.)

What happened after the prophets of Baal tried *all day* to get their god to light the fire on their altar? (Show on your face what you might have been thinking if you were in the crowd.)

Now it's Elijah's turn. Remember that home team advantage? Elijah pushed it even further. After building his altar to God Almighty, Elijah dug a big trench (like a moat) around the altar. (Show on your face what you might have been thinking if you were in the crowd.)

Then he asked for four jars of water to pour over the wood and meat. This made it wet so it would be harder to catch fire and burn. *Three times* they dumped all that water on the drought-dried wood on the altar. It became so wet that the extra water filled the trench Elijah had dug. (Show on your face what you might have been thinking if you were in the crowd.)

Finally, Elijah was ready.

Read 1 Kings 18:36–38. (Show on your face what you might have been thinking if you were in the crowd.)

Read 1 Kings 18:39. (Show on your face what you might have been thinking if you were in the crowd.)

Elijah challenged the people to choose which God they would serve. They saw for themselves that God Almighty is the true God. We, too, have to decide who we will worship and serve. Other people will try to tell us to worship who they worship. We need to know for sure why we believe God is real. We can have a relationship with God Almighty, a God who is real. That is why we study the Bible and pray. Do you have a relationship with Him?

Week 2: Application Activities

Do at least one of the following activities.

On the Road Family Challenge Review

Younger and Older Kids: God's Word tells us what is true.

Supplies Needed: Blindfold, large garbage bag, variety of objects

Advanced Preparation: Hide the objects in the garbage bag before the group arrives.

Grab a blindfold and a variety of objects (stuffed animal, pot, hat, book, mug, sports equipment, a closed purse, one shoe, a puzzle piece, a marker, etc.). *Let only one person see the objects in question.* Hide them in a suitcase, under the table, in the kitchen cabinet, or wherever you like.

Take turns blindfolding each other. The person who knows what the objects are should place one object into the hands of the blindfolded person. That person should use his or her hands, ears, nose, and possibly tongue to describe as much as possible about the object to the rest of the family (who can see it but can't say anything). Try to describe how the object looks and its color, too. If you don't know, guess. When finished, take off the blindfold and start again with someone else.

Questions for each person:

What were the easiest things to know about the object you held? (Or for young children, what did you know about your object without looking?)

What could you not possibly know about your object without looking at it? (For young children, what did you know about someone else's object that he or she didn't?)

We can't always see the big picture, but God can. That is why we turn to God's Word to find the answers to our questions.

Treasure Map

Younger and Older Kids: God's Word tells us what is true.

Supplies Needed: Paper, markers, crayons, maps or magazines to cut up (optional), scissors (optional), glue (optional)

Have people work in small groups or teams to create treasure maps. Include pictures of landmarks someone following the map will see along the way and a big X to mark the spot.

As you work, discuss treasure maps.

Have groups share the adventure people will have following their maps. What kinds of things will they see along the way? What treasure will they find at the end?

How would you feel if you went on a treasure hunt? Remind families of adventure stories like *Treasure Island* or *Treasure Planet*. Do treasure maps always show us exactly what we might experience if we follow them? The maps give us some idea of what to expect, but they don't give us the whole picture of the adventure to come.

God's Word gives us the directions we need to follow God and receive a great treasure in heaven, but there is so much more to the adventure when we start to live it out. If we stop following the treasure map and go our own way, would we find the treasure at the end? The same thing is true of the map God's Word gives for the way to heaven. God says believing and trusting in Jesus' death and resurrection is the only way to get to heaven. Any other way may be a great adventure, but it won't get you to the prize at the end.

Is It True?

Younger and Older Kids: God's Word tells us what is true.

Supplies Needed: Picture of a Bible, picture of a frowning face

Advanced Preparation: Put a picture of a Bible on one wall and a picture of a frown on the opposite wall.

Some people say we cannot know if something is really true or not. We are going to play a game to test and see if we can know if something is really true. Read the following statements. (Feel free to add your own.) Instruct people to move to the Bible if the statement is true and to the frown if it is not.

- Cats fly.
- 2 + 2 = 4
- The sky is green.
- God loves me.
- I like my friends.
- Kangaroos hop.
- 1 + 3 = 10
- God's truth never changes.

- The Bible tells me what God says.
- Fish swim.
- The Bible is true.
- I write with my right hand.
- My friends always have and always will tell me the truth.
- I am wearing __ (color).

So what do you think? Can we know for sure if something is true or not?
What are some ways we know God's Word is true?

Week 2: Wrap It Up

Younger and Older Kids: God's Word tells us what is true.

For the word of God is alive and active. Sharper than any double-edged sword, it penetrates even to dividing soul and spirit, joints and marrow; it judges the thoughts and attitudes of the heart. Nothing in all creation is hidden from God's sight. Everything is uncovered and laid bare before the eyes of him to whom we must give account. (Hebrews 4:11–13 NIV)

God knows everything. He also knows what is true and what is not, what is right and what is wrong. He tells us in His Word—the Bible—so we can know, too. Whenever we have a question, we just need to ask Him and search God's Word. Other people can help you if you need it. God will help us find the answer.

What have you learned about God that you can share with someone else this week?

Week 2: Prayer Focus

Younger and Older Kids: God's Word tells us what is true.

But in your hearts revere Christ as Lord. Always be prepared to give an answer to everyone who asks you to give the reason for the hope that you have. But do this with gentleness and respect. (1 Peter 3:15 NIV).

At some point, someone will either ask us what we believe, why we believe it, or challenge what we believe. We may even wonder why the Bible says the things it does. God encourages us to look for the answers to our questions, so we can know them for ourselves and be able to share them with others. Are there any praises or prayer requests this week?

End your prayer time thanking God that His Word is true. Ask Him to help you find the answers to your questions in the Bible.

Week 3: Why Spend Time With God?

This is what God wants most from you: a relationship!
It's the most astounding truth in the universe—
that our Creator wants to fellowship with us.
God made you to love you, and he longs for you to love him back.

Rick Warren[12]

Main Point (Say this a lot today.)

> *Younger Kids:* God loves us.
> *Older Kids:* God wants a relationship with us.

Scripture

The gospel—2 Corinthians 5:21 (see also Genesis 3:8; Romans 3:23; Romans 6:23; 1 John 1:9; John 1:12)
Reasons to pray—James 5:13–16
Abide in the Vine—John 15:5–8

Prepare Your Heart to Teach

When was the last time you read God's Word and rested in His presence?

It's easy to get caught up in the busyness of life and wake up ready to tackle long to-do lists. Before you know it, another day is gone, and there just wasn't time for personal Bible reading.

God is still there. He's waiting for us to come to Him. He has promised to never leave us or forsake us (Joshua 1:5; Hebrews 13:5).

> Because of the Lord's great love we are not consumed,
>   for his compassions never fail.
> They are new every morning;
>   great is your faithfulness.

I say to myself, "The LORD is my portion;
therefore I will wait for him." (Lamentations 3:22–24 NIV)

Take time to rest in Him today.

Week 3: Opening Activity (optional)

Do at least one of the following activities.

My Bible Book Song

Younger Kids: God loves us.
Older Kids: God wants a relationship with us.

Feel free to repeat previous Bible activities or find more ideas at *www.MrMarksClassroom.com*.

Supplies Needed: Paper; pencils, pens, markers; complete Bibles (i.e., not just New Testaments), timekeeping device (clock, stopwatch)

Advance Preparation (optional): Make a list of the books of the Old Testament, and place it where it can be seen by all.

There are five books in the middle of the Bible that we call the books of Wisdom or Poetry. They are Job, Psalms, Proverbs, Ecclesiastes, and Song of Songs (which is also called Song of Solomon or Canticles). Say those really slowly with me: Job (rhymes with ode), Psalms, Pro-verbs, Ec-cle-si-as-tes, Song of Songs. (You may choose to say Song of Solomon or Canticles.) Now say it a little faster … a little faster. Now really fast. Now regular speed one more time. Good.

Psalms is a large book of songs located in the middle of the Bible. Let's practice finding it. Hold the closed Bible in your hands, and look at the pages pressed together. Try to open it in the very middle. You should be in Psalms or very close to it. Did you find it? Practice it a few more times.

Since Psalms is a book of songs, you are going to write your own song, poem, or rap. Use the names of the books of the Bible in your song. Remember that the books are listed in order in the table of contents in the front of the Bible. (You may choose to break the group into pairs or teams if you wish.) You only have ____ minutes to finish before you will share your creation with the group. Go!

What Do You Know?

Younger Kids: God loves us.
Older Kids: God wants a relationship with us.

Supplies Needed: A loud timer and/or timekeeper

Caution: There is a *secret twist* in this activity.

Have learners pair up with someone they do not know very well. Explain that each person will be given a specific amount of time to learn all they can about their partner to share with the group. Their job is to become an expert about their partner and learn all they can in in the time given. When time is up, they will share with the group all they learned (and remember) about their partner. Teams should decide who will talk first.

Unless you have learners who need to know in advance (e.g., kids on the autism spectrum), do not tell the groups how long each partner will have to talk or listen. Just cut them off when the time is up.

Give the first partner thirty seconds, and allow groups to share what they learned. Give the second partner five seconds (yes, five seconds), and allow groups to share what they learned.

Which partner had a harder time? Why?

Which partner learned more about his or her teammate? Why?

Do you think we learn more about people the more time we spend with them? Why or why not?

When we spend time with God, we get to know Him better. That is why we read the Bible, pray, and worship God—to get to know Him better. The more time we spend doing those things, the better we get to know God.

Music

Younger Kids: God loves us.
Older Kids: God wants a relationship with us.

Supplies Needed: A willingness to worship God through singing (Did I say sing well? Children just need someone to lead them. They are not critics.), CD and player (optional), computer with speakers (optional), DVD and player (optional), phone with music player (optional), instrument with player and music (optional)

Advanced Preparation: Choose the songs and how you will lead them.

Following you will find a variety of songs and styles. Please do not try to do them all. If you choose to do music, I recommend learning three to four songs over the course of the next seven weeks. Choose what works best for your group. For children, I would choose mostly fast songs and end with one slower, worshipful song. You decide what that means for your group. Feel free to change the order of the categories listed below. These songs may be found on *YouTube* and may be purchased on *iTunes* or CD. Some are also available on DVD.

God's Word Is the Source of Truth
   "Jesus Loves Me" (There are lots of variations of this, for example, "Hey! Jesus Loves Me!" "Jesus Loves Me Rock")
   There are several books of the Bible songs and raps. One puts the books to the tune of "Ten Little Indians."
   "The Wise Man and the Foolish Man" ("The wise man built his house upon the rock …")
   "Wonderful Words of Life," by Philip P. Bliss

Who God Is
   "Better Is One Day," by Matt Redman or Kutless
   "My God Is so Big"
   "One Way," by Hillsong Kids
   "Tell Me the Stories of Jesus," by Parker and Challinor

God Loves Me
   "Amazing Grace" (or "My Chains Are Gone," by Chris Tomlin)
   "He Knows My Name," by Maranatha Singers
   "Get Down," by Audio Adrenaline
   "Supernatural," by Hillsong Kids

Week 3: Bible Focus (optional[7])

Younger Kids: God loves us.
Older Kids: God wants a relationship with us.

Supplies Needed: None

God made us to have a relationship with Him. Adam and Eve lived in a perfect relationship with God in the Garden of Eden.[13] Sin separates us from God (Romans 3:23), but Jesus paid the price for our sin (Romans 6:23). Now, if we turn from our sin, tell God we're truly sorry, and trust Jesus as our Lord and Savior, we can have new life and a relationship with God our Father (1 John 1:9; John 1:12).

Think of someone you know really well. Give a thumbs-up if the statement I read is something you do with that person and thumbs-down if you don't.

- talk to that person
- avoid that person
- know what that person likes or doesn't like
- ignore that person
- spend time with that person
- do things for that person
- like or love that person
- hurt that person on purpose

The things most (or all) of you gave thumbs-up for are part of a relationship. We make that relationship stronger when we spend time with God, reading the Bible, praying, and worshipping and serving Him.

There are lots of reasons to pray (James 5:13–16).

- You may be happy. Show me your happy face. This is a good time to praise God.
- You may be in trouble. Show me your scared face. This is a good time to ask God for help.
- You may be sick. Show me an "I don't feel good" face. This is a good time to ask God to heal you and make you better.
- Maybe you made a bad choice and sinned. Show me your "I messed up" face. That is the time to tell God you're sorry and ask Him to forgive you.

Because of Jesus we can be forgiven. Second Corinthians 5:21 (NIV) says, "God made him who had no sin [Jesus] to be sin for us, so that in him we might become the righteousness of God [so we can be forgiven]."

This is the start of that relationship with God. We grow in that relationship by spending time with God, reading the Bible, praying, and worshipping and serving Him. John 15 calls this, "abiding in the vine." Read John 15:5–8.

What are some ways we can abide in the Vine? How can you spend time with God this week?

Week 3: Application Activities

Do at least one of the following activities.

On the Road Family Challenge Review

Younger Kids: God loves us.
Older Kids: God Wants a relationship with us.

Supplies Needed: A timer or a clock with a second hand

You practiced this at home as a family, now try it in mixed groups. Challenge everyone to grab a partner—someone they don't usually spend a lot of time with or don't know very well. (Younger children and a parent can count as one person in a pair if that would make them more comfortable.) Now grab another partner set (or two or three) and complete the challenge.

Have everyone sit in a circle. Put young children next to adults, teenagers, or older children, who can help them with ideas if they get stuck.

Set a timer for thirty seconds, and see how many things you can name to be thankful for about God, things He's done for you or given to you. Take turns around the circle. See how far you can get around the circle (or how many times around) before time is up. When time is up, have everyone say together, "Thank You, God, for loving us!" This can be in response to a timer or echoing the timekeeper's loud, "Thank You, God, for loving us!" Now you're on a roll. Set the timer and go again! This time, start at a different place in the circle, change topics, or try to get further around the circle.

Topics to get you started:

- who God is
- things God has made (especially good for toddlers and younger children)
- things God has done
- people and things God has given you

Emotion Turnaround

Younger Kids: God loves us.
Older Kids: God wants a relationship with us.

33

Supplies Needed per family group: Two large paper plates (the plastic ones will be much harder to cut); one brass fastener; markers, crayons, pens, or pencils; scissors

Advanced Preparation: Make a sample. Precut the paper plates according to the instructions below (optional).

Read together Philippians 4:4–9 (MSG):

> Celebrate God all day, every day. I mean, revel in him! Make it as clear as you can to all you meet that you're on their side, working with them and not against them. Help them see that the Master is about to arrive. He could show up any minute!

> Don't fret or worry. Instead of worrying, pray. Let petitions and praises shape your worries into prayers, letting God know your concerns. Before you know it, a sense of God's wholeness, everything coming together for good, will come and settle you down. It's wonderful what happens when Christ displaces worry at the center of your life.

> Summing it all up, friends, I'd say you'll do best by filling your minds and meditating on things true, noble, reputable, authentic, compelling, gracious—the best, not the worst; the beautiful, not the ugly; things to praise, not things to curse. Put into practice what you learned from me, what you heard and saw and realized. Do that, and God, who makes everything work together, will work you into his most excellent harmonies.

It is not always easy to praise God, but it can help us to think about God when we are worried or feel sad, angry, or upset. God loves us. Having a relationship with Him means telling Him when we feel bad and asking Him to help us feel better. Part of how we do that is to focus on God, not our problems. Let's make a wheel to remind us to think of God and pray and praise Him, no matter how we feel.

On the back of one plate, lightly draw a large X, dividing the plate into quarters. Then draw a circle dividing the plate into two nestled circles. Cut out one quarter in the outer ring and an opposite outer quarter (see example). Be sure to leave enough space in the center for the brass fastener to hold this plate to the complete plate below. Nestle the two plates so the drawn lines do not show and attach with the brass fastener.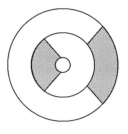

In the smaller inner opening, draw a happy face. In the larger outer space, draw a reason to praise God when you're happy. Then turn the top plate a quarter turn and do the same thing with a sad face, giving a reason to praise God when you are sad. Then move the plate a quarter turn and draw an excited face. What reasons would you have to praise God when you are excited? You choose what the fourth face should look like. How can you praise God in that situation?

Lighten Your Burden

Younger Kids: God loves us.
Older Kids: God wants a relationship with us.

Supplies Needed: Four buckets, two sturdy cups, something to fill the buckets (e.g., water if done outside, beans, small blocks, bean bags, etc.)

Before your relay race, ask one child to try to pick up one of the full buckets. Is it heavy? Then allow others to help lift the bucket. Is that easier?

Take out some of what's inside the bucket. For each answer to the following question, put some of it back into the bucket. What are some things that weigh us down, making us sad, angry, upset, worried, or scared?

Read Matthew 11:28–30 (NIV): "Come to me, all you who are weary and burdened, and I will give you rest. Take my yoke upon you and learn from me, for I am gentle and humble in heart, and you will find rest for your souls. For my yoke is easy and my burden is light."

God loves us and wants to help us with our fears, worries, upsets, and other burdens. One way He lifts our burdens and helps us is when we pray. Prayer is talking to God. When we pray, we strengthen our relationship with God. We also remind ourselves that God loves us very much and will take care of us, no matter what. When we remember these things, our fears, upsets, and worries seem lighter. Let's play a game to see how this works.

Divide the group into two teams. Place an empty bucket across the room from each team and the full bucket at the front of each team's line. In this relay race, each person in line should take one cupful of what is in the full bucket, run down and put it in the bucket across the room, return, give the cup to the next person, and go to the back of the line.

When you finish the game, have the same child lift the same bucket you did at the beginning. Is it as heavy as before? Why? God wants to help lighten our burdens, too.

Week 3: Wrap It Up

Younger Kids: God loves us.
Older Kids: God wants a relationship with us.

Praise the LORD.
Give thanks to the LORD, for he is good;
> his love endures forever. (Psalm 106:1 NIV)

It's easy to forget how good God is, but God loves us and wants to have a relationship with us. When we spend time reading the Bible, praying, and worshipping Him, we help that relationship to grow.

What is one way you can remember to spend time with God this week? (For younger children: What is one way you can remember that God loves you?)

Week 3: Prayer Focus

Younger Kids: God loves us.
Older Kids: God wants a relationship with us.

You're blessed when you stay on course,
> walking steadily on the road revealed by God.
You're blessed when you follow his directions,
> doing your best to find him. (Psalm 119:1–2 MSG)

God loves us. He wants us to trust Him and His Word. He takes good care of us. Are there any special prayer requests this week?

End your prayer time thanking God for His love and asking Him to help you want to spend more time reading the Bible, praying, and worshipping the Lord.

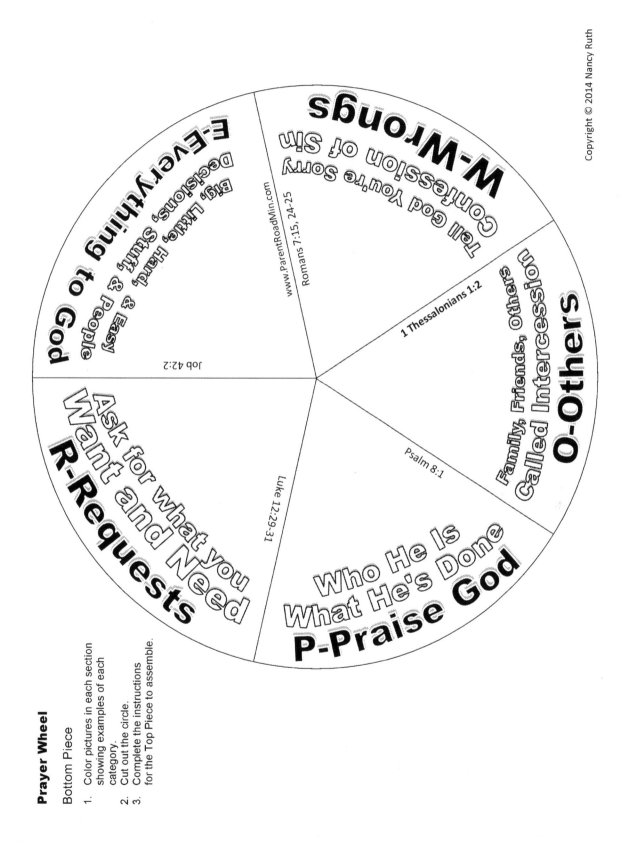

Prayer Wheel

Bottom Piece

1. Color pictures in each section showing examples of each category.
2. Cut out the circle.
3. Complete the instructions for the Top Piece to assemble.

(Content within the wheel:)

E-Everything to God
Big, Little, Hard, Stuff & Easy Decisions, Stuff & People
Job 42:2

W-Wrongs
Confession of Sin
Tell God You're Sorry
Romans 7:15, 24-25
www.ParentRoadMin.com

O-Others
Called Intercession
Family, Friends, Others
1 Thessalonians 1:2

P-Praise God
What He's Done
Who He Is
Psalm 8:1

R-Requests
Want and Need
Ask for what you
Luke 12:29-31

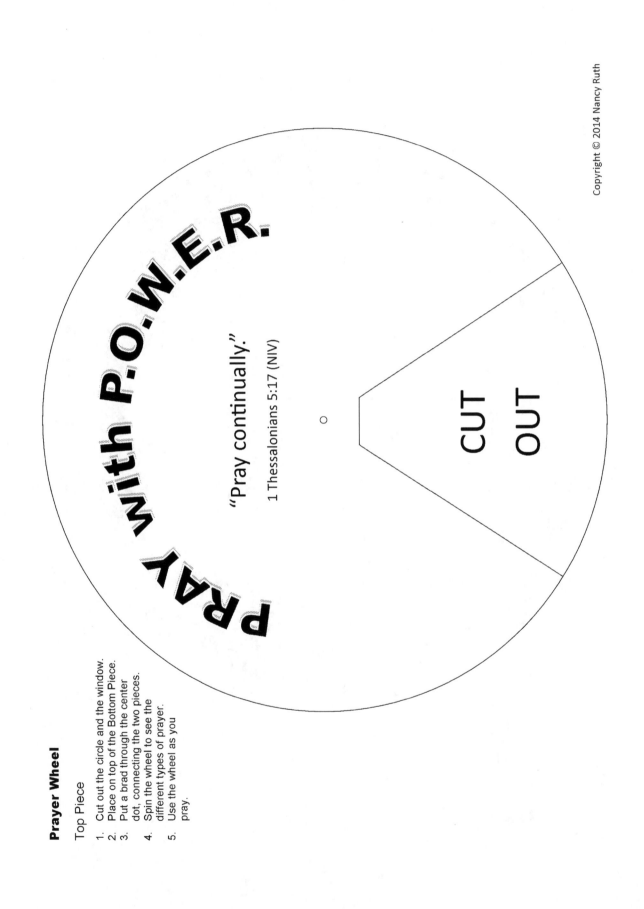

Prayer Wheel

Top Piece

1. Cut out the circle and the window.
2. Place on top of the Bottom Piece.
3. Put a brad through the center dot, connecting the two pieces.
4. Spin the wheel to see the different types of prayer.
5. Use the wheel as you pray.

PRAY with P.O.W.E.R.

"Pray continually."
1 Thessalonians 5:17 (NIV)

CUT
OUT

Week 4: Who Are the People God Can Use?

> Don't let what's wrong with you
> keep you from worshiping
> what's right with God.
>
> Mark Batterson[14]

Main Point (Say this a lot today.)

Younger and Older Kids: God can use anyone who follows Jesus.

Scripture

God chose Gideon to free Israel from the Midianites (pronounced "MID-ee-uhn-ites"). See Judges 6:1–24; 7.

Prepare Your Heart to Teach

What keeps you from feeling worthy to be used by God?

> I praise you because I am fearfully and wonderfully made; your works are wonderful, I know that full well … your eyes saw my unformed body. All the days ordained for me were written in your book before one of them came to be. (Psalm 139:14, 16 NIV)

God chose you. He made you, and He loves you. Christ died for your sins. In Him you can have new life. In His strength, you—like Gideon—are called to do great works for the Lord's glory. God can use anyone who follows Jesus.

> For we are God's workmanship, created in Christ Jesus to do good works, which God prepared in advance for us to do. (Ephesians 2:10 NIV)

Week 4: Opening Activity (optional)

Do at least one of the following activities.

Rough Books

Younger and Older Kids: God can use anyone who follows Jesus.

Feel free to repeat previous Bible activities or find more ideas at *www.MrMarksClassroom.com.*

Supplies Needed: A list of the books from Isaiah to Malachi, or all the Bible books; sandpaper, sandbox, or another rough surface (like rocks or dirt)

Say together the names of all the Old Testament Prophets. Be sure to start slowly, especially for the longer names.

I-sa-iah	E-ze-ki-el	Joel	Jo-nah	Ha-bak-kuk	Zech-a-ri-ah
Jer-e-mi-ah	Dan-iel	A-mos	Mi-cah	Ze-pha-ni-ah	Mal-a-chi
Lam-en-ta-tions	Ho-se-a	O-ba-di-ah	Na-hum	Hag-ga-i	

Have everyone write the first letter or the whole name of each of the Old Testament prophets on the rough surface in order as you say them together. When you finish, say the whole list again.

Times were rough in the days of the Old Testament prophets. The people of Israel had forgotten the Lord and His Word. The prophets tried to warn them to repent of their sins and turn back to God. If they didn't, they would be punished. The people did not listen, and God punished them, just as He said He would. It was a very rough time for the prophets to live and speak for God because most of the people around them were not. The prophets were not born different than anyone else around them. What made them special enough for us to remember them today was the fact that they followed God when most others did not. God used them in mighty ways. God can use anyone who follows Jesus—even you. Name the Old Testament prophets one more time.

Someone Important

Younger and Older Kids: God can use anyone who follows Jesus.

Supplies Needed: Paper and pencils/markers or whiteboard/poster board and markers

Either break into teams (give each person their own paper and writing utensils) or do this as a large group.

If you had to trust someone with an important job, what would you want that person to be like? Your goal is to either make a list of characteristics or draw a picture of this person. Get very specific. Would he or she be strong or weak? Would the person be young, old, or very old? Would it matter if he or she were a boy or a girl? Would it matter what that person did for a living? What would the individual look like? Would anything else be important?

Guess what? God has an important job for us to do, and He only looks for one qualification—a heart that loves Him and is willing to do what He asks. God can use anyone who follows Jesus.

Music

Younger and Older Kids: God can use anyone who follows Jesus.

Supplies Needed: A willingness to worship God through singing (Did I say sing well? Children just need someone to lead them. They are not critics.), CD and player (optional), computer with speakers (optional), DVD and player (optional), phone with music player (optional), instrument with player and music (optional).

Advanced Preparation: Choose the songs and how you will lead them.

Following you will find a variety of songs and styles. Please do not try to do them all. If you choose to do music, I recommend learning three to four songs over the course of the next seven weeks. Choose what works best for your group. For children, I would choose mostly fast songs and end with one slower, worshipful song. You decide what that means for your group. Feel free to change the order of the categories listed below. These songs may be found on *YouTube* and may be purchased on *iTunes* or CD. Some are also available on DVD.

God's Word Is the Source of Truth
    "Jesus Loves Me" (There are lots of variations of this, for example, "Hey! Jesus Loves Me!" "Jesus Loves Me Rock")
    There are several books of the Bible songs and raps. One puts the books to the tune of "Ten Little Indians."
    "The Wise Man and the Foolish Man" ("The wise man built his house upon the rock …")
    "Wonderful Words of Life," by Philip P. Bliss

Who God Is
    "Better Is One Day," by Matt Redman or Kutless
    "My God Is so Big"

"One Way," by Hillsong Kids

"Tell Me the Stories of Jesus," by Parker and Challinor

God Loves Me

"Amazing Grace" (or "My Chains Are Gone," by Chris Tomlin)

"He Knows My Name," by Maranatha Singers

"Get Down," by Audio Adrenaline

"Supernatural," by Hillsong Kids

Week 4: Bible Focus (optional[7])

Younger and Older Kids: God can use anyone who follows Jesus.

Supplies Needed: Bible to teach from; whiteboard, poster board, or large piece of paper; markers

Advanced Preparation (optional): Bookmark Judges 6:2 in your teaching Bible.

Every one of us has a story to tell about the things that have happened in our lives. Some people's stories are recorded in the Bible. Gideon was a man who lived a little over three thousand years ago.[15] Part of his life story is recorded in the history book of Judges in the Bible, chapters 6–8. God had a very important job for Gideon to do. His people were under attack, and God needed someone to save them. As we listen to some of that story today, let's make a list of some of the ways Gideon is described.

Judges 6:2–6 describe the enemy that invaded Gideon's home. (Read these verses together from your teaching Bible. You may choose to look them up as a group or read them yourself. You might take this opportunity to remind learners how to find the book of Judges as you find the verses. Judges is the seventh book of the Bible. First comes the five books of the Law—Genesis, Exodus, Leviticus, Numbers, and Deuteronomy. Next is Joshua and Judges.)

What does "impoverished" mean? Write "Gideon was poor" and "Gideon was in trouble" on your list.

Read Judges 6:11. Here is where Gideon begins his conversation with an angel of the Lord. What two things do we learn about Gideon from this verse? "He is a farmer." "He is creative." (He threshed wheat in the winepress to hide it from the enemy who would have taken it.)

Read verse 12. Wait, I thought Gideon was a farmer.[16] Does Gideon's occupation matter to God?

Read verse 13. Does Gideon sound like he knows God's Word and promises? Make a note on your list.

Does Gideon sound confident? Make a note on your list.

Does it sound like this is a good time for Gideon? Why or why not? Make a note on your list.

Read verse 14. Why will Gideon succeed?

Gideon was part of the nation of Israel. Israel was divided into twelve tribes, kind of like the United States used to be divided into thirteen colonies. Each tribe had its own land, but they sometimes helped each other out. Together they were one country. Gideon's tribe was Manasseh (pronounced "man-AS-eh"). Say that together—Manasseh. The twelve tribes of Israel were also one big family. Of all the tribes, Manasseh was the lowest. You might say Manasseh was like the kid always picked last for games.

Listen to what Gideon says about his family. Read verse 15.

What did Gideon say about his family?

Was Gideon an important man? Make a note on your list.

Did that matter to God?

Read verses 17 through 24.

Look at your list again. Did Gideon make an ideal hero for people in trouble?

God used Gideon because he followed God and was willing to do what God said. Gideon did great things for God and freed his people, because he was willing to do what God said (Judges 7).

God can use you, too. Are you willing to follow God and do what He says?

Week 4: Application Activities

Do at least one of the following activities.

On the Road Family Challenge Review

Younger and Older Kids: God can use anyone who follows Jesus.

Supplies Needed: A Bible

Gather the family and read the following verses (use the table of contents or *www.biblegateway.com* if needed): Hebrews 11:1–2, 4–7, 17–26, 40. Then ask everyone this question: If you were anyone in the Bible, who would you be and why?

Questions for each person.

If you were anyone in the Bible, who would you be and why? (Or, for young children, What is your favorite Bible story?)

Once everyone has shared, choose one or more of the Bible stories mentioned to act out together.

Follow the Leader

Younger and Older Kids: God can use anyone who follows Jesus.

Supplies Needed: None

Play a game of Follow the Leader. After you play for a while, stop to talk a bit before playing some more.

Remind the group that we look up to people we admire and try to follow their examples. Toddlers look up to younger kids, younger kids look up to older kids, older kids look up to teenagers, teenagers look up to adults, and adults look up to older adults. Older adults look up to others, too, but sometimes those people have already passed away.

With all these people looking for someone's example to follow, someone will be looking to you to follow your example. What kind of example are you setting for others to follow? Are you pointing others to Jesus through your words and actions? What are some ways we can show others Jesus by the way we live?

My Hero

Younger and Older Kids: God can use anyone who follows Jesus.

Supplies Needed: Paper, pencils, markers, or crayons; stickers (optional); colored paper (optional)

Read together Hebrews 11:1–2; 12:1 (NIV): "Now faith is confidence in what we hope for and assurance about what we do not see. This is what the ancients were commended for … Therefore, since we are surrounded by such a great cloud of witnesses, let us throw off everything that hinders and the sin that so easily entangles. And let us run with perseverance the race marked out for us."

Who shows you best how to live for Jesus? Who is your "hero of the faith"? Why do you look up to this person? How does his or her example help you live your life for Jesus? Draw a picture of you and that person. Write a letter or thank you note to give them.

Week 4: Wrap It Up

Younger and Older Kids: God can use anyone who follows Jesus.

Don't let anyone look down on you because you are young, but set an example for the believers in speech, in life, in love, in faith and in purity. (1 Timothy 4:12 NIV)

Just as the Bible gives us good examples to follow, younger brothers and sisters and other people look at us for how to live.

What are some ways you can be a good example to others?

Week 4: Prayer Focus

Younger and Older Kids: God can use anyone who follows Jesus.

Join with others in following my example, brothers and take note of those who live according to the pattern we gave you. (Philippians 3:17 NIV)

The Bible gave us lots of good examples of men and women who followed God in all they did. Are there any special praises or prayer requests this week?

End your prayer time asking God to help you be a good example to other believers.

Week 5: Who Is Jesus?

Either this man was, and is, the Son of God:
or else a madman or something worse.
You can shut Him up for a fool, you can spit at Him and kill Him as a demon;
or you can fall at His feet and call Him Lord and God.
But let us not come with any patronizing nonsense
about His being a great human teacher.

C. S. Lewis[17]

Main Point (Say this a lot today.)

Younger and Older Kids: The Bible tells the truth about Jesus.

Scripture

Jesus' Day of Interruptions—Mark 5

Prepare Your Heart to Teach

There was a lot of confusion about who Jesus was when He walked the earth. Some thought He was a prophet. Some thought He was Elijah or John the Baptist come back to life. Jesus discussed this with His disciples. Then He asked them, "Who do you say that I am?" (Matthew 16:13–16).

How would you answer that question? Who is Jesus? Could you quickly and confidently reply with Peter, "You are the Messiah, the Son of the living God" (Matthew 16:17 NIV)? Or would you let someone else answer first?

Ask God to answer your questions and doubts, clearly showing you who Jesus truly is. (See John 20:19–31.)

If you already know Him, ask Him to teach you more about Him and show you who else you can tell about Him.

Week 5: Opening Activity (optional)

Do at least one of the following activities

Ready, Set, Gospel!

Younger and Older Kids: The Bible tells the truth about Jesus.

Feel free to repeat previous Bible activities or find more ideas at *www.MrMarksClassroom.com.*

Supplies Needed: Bibles, circle of chairs or seats (one per person, less one), individual cards for the books. Today we're using Genesis through John (see *www.sundayschoolsources.com/books-bible-bingo.htm* for premade cards), list or poster of all the Bible books (optional)

Advanced Preparation: You will not need all the Bible book cards, but you will need some from at least three divisions of the Bible, including the Gospels and New Testament History (Acts).

Practice opening the Bible in the middle to find Psalms. Open the right half in the middle to find the Gospels, which are at the beginning of the New Testament.

Review several times the names of the four Gospels: Matthew, Mark, Luke, John. Review the other Bible divisions you are using in the game (see advanced preparation notes).

Choose one person to be "It." Distribute the books of the Bible cards you will be using (see advanced preparation notes) to each person, including It. It stands in the middle, while everyone else is seated in the circle. It calls out a division of the Bible. It and anyone holding a book in that division must find a seat. The person left standing is the new It.

Multiple Portraits

Younger and Older Kids: The Bible tells the truth about Jesus.

Supplies Needed: Paper and markers or crayons or Play-Doh.

Describe the following animals. Challenge learners to draw or mold the animal they think it is while you talk. After each description, ask each learner what animal they thought it was. Did each learner come up with the same creature? Were their drawings or creations match? How were they the same? How were they different? Play again.

Hint: Read the riddles slowly to give learners time to create and modify their answers.

For younger children, simply name the animal and have each one draw or make it. Compare the different creations. How were they the same? How were they different?

1. I eat my food whole
    To the ground I keep low
    I have no eyelids
    My tongue is what smellsssss
    What am I?
    (Snake)

2. For twelve hours I eat
    Bamboo is my treat
    My fur's black and white
    All the kids I delight
    What am I?
    (Panda Bear)

3. I carry my home
    Never far do I roam
    When rain comes I am seen
    I am not known for my speed
    What am I?
    (Snail)

4. I love garden veggies
    And have lots of babies
    My ears hear a lot
    And I love to hop
    What am I?
    (Rabbit)

After playing awhile, gather the troops to discuss.

We had lots of different pictures of these animals, because everyone had a different idea of what they looked like. Does that mean the animals themselves were different? Was the snake really an elephant? No, we just had different people showing us different things about the snake.

Did you know there are four different pictures of Jesus in the Bible? We call them the four Gospels. God helped four of Jesus' followers write down who Jesus was and what He did, so we would know from people who knew Him and spent time with Him—like you do with your friends. Each gospel has things that are the same as the others, because they describe the same man. Some things, though, are different, because different people are describing Jesus. I bet if different people described you, they would each say some things the same and some things a little differently, too. Isn't God good to give us four pictures of Jesus instead of just one? Wow! Now we can know even more about Him.

If you have time, play the game again. Let kids make up their own clues.

Music

Younger and Older Kids: The Bible tells the truth about Jesus.

Supplies Needed: A willingness to worship God through singing (Did I say sing well? Children just need someone to lead them. They are not critics.), CD and player (optional), computer with speakers (optional), DVD and player (optional), phone with music player (optional), instrument with player and music (optional)

Advanced Preparation: Choose the songs and how you will lead them.

Following you will find a variety of songs and styles. Please do not try to do them all. If you choose to do music, I recommend learning three to four songs over the course of the next seven weeks. Choose what works best for your group. For children, I would choose mostly fast songs and end with one slower, worshipful song. You decide what that means for your group. Feel free to change the order of the categories listed below. These songs may be found on *YouTube* and may be purchased on *iTunes* or CD. Some are also available on DVD.

God's Word Is the Source of Truth
 "Jesus Loves Me" (There are lots of variations of this, for example, "Hey! Jesus Loves Me!" "Jesus Loves Me Rock")
 There are several books of the Bible songs and raps. One puts the books to the tune of "Ten Little Indians."
 "The Wise Man and the Foolish Man" ("The wise man built his house upon the rock …")
 "Wonderful Words of Life," by Philip P. Bliss

Who God Is
 "Better Is One Day," by Matt Redman or Kutless
 "My God Is so Big"
 "One Way," by Hillsong Kids
 "Tell Me the Stories of Jesus," by Parker and Challinor

God Loves Me
 "Amazing Grace" (or "My Chains Are Gone," by Chris Tomlin)
 "He Knows My Name," by Maranatha Singers
 "Get Down," by Audio Adrenaline
 "Supernatural," by Hillsong Kids

Week 5: Bible Focus (optional[7])

Younger and Older Kids: The Bible tells the truth about Jesus.

Supplies Needed: Space to move about the room (see "Advanced Preparation")

Advanced Preparation: Start with the group sitting in one corner of the room. You will be moving from corner to corner around the room, ending in the center of the room. If this is not possible, find five other areas that will work, and think through how you will make your journey (boat, first shore, opposite shore, on the road, Jairus's house). It might be fun to move down the hallway or from room to room.

Today we are going to take a journey with Jesus through one day as we try to find out who He really is. The day started with Jesus and His disciples landing their boat on the shore of the lake (Mark 4:35; 5:1). Everyone out of the boat. (Move clockwise to the next corner.)

On the shore, Jesus met a man everyone avoided. This man lived alone in a graveyard and acted crazy, because he had an evil spirit. Read Mark 5:6–8.

When Jesus cast out the evil spirits in the man, they went into two thousand pigs, which ran off a cliff and died. The man, however, was set free. Read Mark 5:14–15.

The people were afraid, because they had never seen anyone like Jesus before. They asked Him to leave. Everyone back in the boat (to that corner) and to the other shore (counterclockwise).

A large crowd greeted Jesus there. Read Mark 5:22–23.

Jesus agreed to go with Jairus, and a large crowd followed them. (Move counterclockwise to the next corner.)

How many of you have walked in a large crowd?
Have you ever accidentally bumped into someone or have someone brush against you?
How often do you think that might happen if your whole school walked together from the school to the church?
Do you think people might have brushed against Jesus as they walked?

One person who bumped into Jesus had a special reason for touching Him. She had been sick for a long time. She'd tried doctors and medicines but had just gotten worse. She knew only Jesus could make her well.

For some reason, the woman decided not to talk to Jesus. Maybe she didn't want to bother Him. Maybe she wasn't sure He would take the time to talk to her or didn't think she was good enough for Him to take the time. Whatever her reasons, she decided there was still a way Jesus could heal her.

Read Mark 5:27–36.

What have we seen Jesus do so far? (Cast out demons and free the man by the shore, heal the woman and free her from her suffering.)

Why should Jairus, the synagogue ruler, not to be afraid? (Because He believes and trusts in Jesus.)

Jesus only let a few of His close disciples follow Him to Jairus's house. Let's see what happened when they got there. Move to the center of the room.

Read Mark 5:38–43. What happened?

Jesus healed people, cast out demons, and brought people back from the dead. Jesus also died on the cross and came back to life again so our sins could be forgiven and we could live with Him (1 Corinthians 15:3–4). Jesus is unlike anyone else who ever lived. He is more than a good man, a prophet, or a good teacher. Jesus is God in a human body (Philippians 2:5–11). Believing in Him is the only way we can have our sins forgiven and live with God in heaven when we die.

(See page 8 if anyone would like to know more about asking Jesus to be his or her Lord and Savior.)

Week 5: Application Activities

Do at least one of the following activities.

On the Road Family Challenge Review

Younger and Older Kids: The Bible tells the truth about Jesus.

Supplies Needed: None

Advanced Preparation: You will need a mediator comfortable leading this discussion.

This is the week to find out where your family stands. Ask your kids, "What do you know about Jesus?" If you're comfortable, follow it up with a conversation. If not, just thank them for sharing, and remember their answer(s) to follow up later.

Questions for each person:

What do you know about Jesus?

Has anyone ever challenged you because of what you believe? (Or for young children, Do you know anyone who does not believe in Jesus or the Bible?)

Jesus Book

Younger and Older Kids: The Bible tells the truth about Jesus.

Supplies Needed: Paper cut into quarters; stapler; crayons, markers, pens, or pencils

Advanced Preparation (optional): Pre-print and cut papers with the labels described below.

Create and assemble booklets with the following pages stapled together. Draw pictures or write the story to go along with each title. You may do this individually, as partners, or in family groups.

1. All about Jesus (title page)
2. Jesus Was Born (Luke 2:1–20)
3. Jesus Was Baptized (Mark 1:9–11)
4. Jesus Healed People (Matthew 9:18–38)
5. Jesus Calmed a Storm (Matthew 8:23–27)
6. Jesus Died on the Cross (John 19)
7. Jesus Rose from the Dead (Luke 24:1–12)
8. Jesus Is Coming Back Someday (Acts 1:7–11)

Tell Me about Jesus

Younger and Older Kids: The Bible tells the truth about Jesus.

Supplies Needed: None

One of the best ways to know how to answer someone who wants to know about Jesus or someone who says something that is different from what the Bible says about Jesus is to practice. Take turns acting out scenarios like the following. (You may also break into teams to plan a skit based on one of the following and then take turns sharing your skits with the whole group.)

- Your friend says their parents say there is no God. What do you say?
- Your friend asks what makes Jesus different from other prophets. What do you say?
- Your friend has never heard of Jesus. Who is He?

- Your friend wants to know how to get to heaven. What do you say?
- Someone asks you why you believe in Jesus. What do you say?
- You tell someone about Jesus, and he or she doesn't believe you. What do you say and do?

Week 5: Wrap It Up

Younger and Older Kids: The Bible tells the truth about Jesus.

For what I received I passed on to you as of first importance: that Christ died for our sins according to the Scriptures, that he was buried, that he was raised on the third day according to the Scriptures. (1 Corinthians 15:3–4 NIV)

The Bible tells us that Jesus is God's Son, who lived a perfect life, died, and rose again to pay for our sins. Any time we hear something different from that or something we are not sure about, all we have to do is check what the Bible says to know what is true.

Where can we go to learn more about Jesus?

Week 5: Prayer Focus

Younger and Older Kids: The Bible tells the truth about Jesus.

We did not follow cleverly invented stories when we told you about the power and coming of our Lord Jesus Christ, but we were eyewitnesses of his majesty. (2 Peter 1:16 NIV)

God is real, and so is Jesus Christ. We have eyewitness accounts of Jesus' life, ministry, and death here on earth as well as reports of those who have had life-changing encounters with Him today. Praise God!

Are there any special praises or prayer requests this week?

End your prayer time thanking God for Jesus Christ.

Week 6: How Can You Be Changed?

In other words, the Christian life is one of faith,
where we find ourselves routinely overdriving our headlights
but knowing it's okay because God is in control
and has a purpose behind it.

Bill Hybels and Mark Mittelberg[18]

Main Point (Say this a lot today.)

Younger and Older Kids: Jesus died for us.

Scripture

The gospel—John 3:16; Romans 3:23; 1 Corinthians 15:3–4; John 11:12

Be sure to share the gospel this week. Do not push for a decision, especially from younger children, but be sensitive to the Holy Spirit's leading. Direct children to their parents if they wish to make a decision, or see page 8 to lead that one-on-one discussion yourself.

Prepare Your Heart to Teach

Did you know that God does not seem to separate "little sins" and "big sins"?

The Old Testament law regulated punishments to keep things more "eye for an eye and a tooth for a tooth" (Leviticus 24:19–21), since the common practice of the world in that day was more like "head for a tooth." Still, Jesus came and told the people God's real heart behind the original commands. Calling someone spiteful names is the same as murder (Matthew 5:21–22). Lust is the same as adultery (Matthew 5:21–22). Disobeying parents is on par with gossip, envy, murder, God-haters, and strife (Romans 1:29–30).

I don't know about you, but that makes me feel pretty low. If that's the standard, there is no way I could ever measure up.

Jesus replied, "Very truly I tell you, everyone who sins is a slave to sin. Now a slave has no permanent place in the family, but a son belongs to it forever. So if the Son sets you free, you will be free indeed" (John 8:34–36 NIV).

Jesus died to set us free from sin. His blood covers all of our sins. All we have to do is confess it and turn to Him in faith. When was the last time you came clean before the Father? Why not take time to do that today?

You can't whitewash your sins and get by with it;
    you find mercy by admitting and leaving them (Proverbs 28:13 MSG)

Week 6: Opening Activity (optional)

Do at least one of the following activities.

What'd You Say?

Younger and Older Kids: Jesus died for us.

Feel free to repeat previous Bible activities or find new ideas at *www.MrMarksClassroom.com*.

Supplies Needed: Blindfold, large garbage bag, variety of objects

The New Testament books called Letters, or Epistles, were originally just that—letters written to churches for them to read aloud to everyone. Once they learned what the letter said, they passed it on to the next church so they could use it, too.

Play telephone, sending three New Testament letter books at a time down the line. As time allows and players get better, send more books at a time. See if they can make it all the way down the line without getting jumbled.

Turn Around

Younger and Older Kids: Jesus died for us.

Feel free to repeat previous Bible activities or find more ideas at *www.MrMarksClassroom.com*.

Supplies Needed: Piece of scrap paper and writing utensil, open space

Line players up against one wall, with the caller against the opposite wall. Leave an open space in between.

Count the number of players (not including the caller). The caller should write a number from 1 to the total number of players (e.g., 3) on a piece of paper, without showing anyone. Fold it, and stand on it to hide it.

Players start facing away from the caller. When the caller says, "Go," players carefully walk backward toward the caller. At any time, the caller may say, "Turn around." Players then turn and walk forward toward the caller. The caller at any time may again say, "Turn around." Players must then turn around and walk backward toward the caller.

Keep track of the order players reach the caller. The number of the player to reach the caller that matches the number the caller wrote on the piece of paper wins and is the new caller.

After playing for a while, gather learners to discuss. Jesus died for each and every one of us. There is nothing we can do to earn His love and forgiveness. The only thing we need to do is to believe in Jesus and turn away from our sin, which means tell God we are really sorry and try not to do it anymore. We're going to learn more about that today. If you have time, play the game again.

Music

Younger and Older Kids: Jesus died for us.

Supplies Needed: A willingness to worship God through singing (Did I say sing well? Children just need someone to lead them. They are not critics.), CD and player (optional), computer with speakers (optional), DVD and player (optional), phone with music player (optional), instrument with player and music (optional)

Advanced Preparation: Choose the songs and how you will lead them.

Following you will find a variety of songs and styles. Please do not try to do them all. If you choose to do music, I recommend learning three to four songs over the course of the next seven weeks. Choose what works best for your group. For children, I would choose mostly fast songs and end with one slower, worshipful song. You decide what that means for your group. Feel free to change the order of the categories listed below. These songs may be found on *YouTube* and may be purchased on *iTunes* or CD. Some are also available on DVD.

God's Word Is the Source of Truth

"Jesus Loves Me" (There are lots of variations of this, for example, "Hey! Jesus Loves Me!" "Jesus Loves Me Rock")

There are several books of the Bible songs and raps. One puts the books to the tune of "Ten Little Indians."

"The Wise Man and the Foolish Man" ("The wise man built his house upon the rock …")

"Wonderful Words of Life," by Philip P. Bliss

Who God Is

"Better Is One Day," by Matt Redman or Kutless

"My God Is so Big"

"One Way," by Hillsong Kids

"Tell Me the Stories of Jesus," by Parker and Challinor

God Loves Me

"Amazing Grace" (or "My Chains Are Gone," by Chris Tomlin)

"He Knows My Name," by Maranatha Singers

"Get Down," by Audio Adrenaline

"Supernatural," by Hillsong Kids

Week 6: Bible Focus (optional[7])

Younger and Older Kids: Jesus died for us.

Feel free to adapt this and weave it into one of the application activities.

Supplies Needed: Some kids have trouble sitting still and listening. If you have people like this in your group, give them paper and something to draw with while you talk. They may surprise you with what they hear while seeming not to pay attention.

Option: Feel free to have children familiar with the gospel share this with you by asking leading questions.

God loves us very much.

> For God so loved the world that he gave his one and only Son, that whoever believes in him shall not perish but have eternal life. (John 3:16 NIV)

Eternal life means living with God in heaven one day. Heaven is God's home. Because God is perfect and good, only perfect and good things can live there.

What are some things that will be in heaven? (Angels, God, Jesus, those who believe in Jesus, throne of God, street of gold, pearly gates, mansion, Tree of Life, Water of Life; see John 14:2; Revelation 5:11; 21:18–21; 22:1–4.)

What are some things that won't be in heaven? (Sin, death, crying, pain, sun, moon, lamps, night, church, or temple; see Revelation 20:14; 21:4; 22:22–23, 25, 27.)

What is sin? (Sin is wrong choices we make in what we do, what we think, and things we say.)

Can you give me some examples of sin?

I know I have made bad choices and sinned. Have you?

> For all have sinned and fall short of the glory of God. (Romans 3:23 NIV)

We've all messed up and done things that disqualify us from getting into heaven. That's a problem, but God provided the answer.

> For God so loved the world that he gave his one and only Son, that whoever believes in him shall not perish but have eternal life. (John 3:16 NIV)

Jesus came and lived life without sinning—not even once!

The punishment for sin is death (Romans 6:23), but when Jesus died on the cross, He didn't die for His sins, because He didn't have any. He died to pay the price for our sins.

All we have to do is accept the gift that Jesus offers us.

First you have to …

A—Admit you are a sinner. That means you have to agree with God that you've made wrong choices and sinned. You tell on yourselves to God and tell Him you're sorry. You also need to turn from those sins by telling God you will try not to do them anymore … and mean it.

The next thing you have to do to accept Jesus' gift is to …

B—*Believe* Jesus died and rose again to pay for your sins.

> For what I received I passed on to you as of first importance: that Christ died for our sins according to the Scriptures,[4] that he was buried, that he was raised on the third day according to the Scriptures. (1 Corinthians 15:3–4 NIV)

Then you have to …

C—*Choose* Jesus to be your Lord and Savior. Savior means He saves us from our sins. Lord means He's our boss. You are choosing to follow Him for the rest of your life.

This is a big decision and not one to be taken lightly. It means that when you are faced with tough decisions, you are now deciding to do what God wants you to do …

even if you really want to do something else.
even if it's hard.
even if your friends want you to do something different.
even if it may cost you.

But know this: God promises it's always worth it in the end.

> Yet to all who did receive him, to those who believed in his name, he gave the right to become children of God. (John 11:12 NIV)

If this is something you would like to do today, please tell your parent. (You may also choose to have children raise hands.)

If you are not ready yet but would like to know more about what all this means, you can talk to your parent about that, too.

If you have already done this, be thinking about who you can share this message with this week.

Week 6: Application Activities

Do at least one of the following activities.

"Tell Me" Bracelet

Younger and Older Kids: Jesus died for us.

Supplies Needed: Suede, hemp, or another thick brown cord (note: some people are allergic to hemp); (2) white, black (or marbled), yellow (or gold), red, and one other color (or a butterfly) pony beads

Advanced Preparation (optional): Precut the suede. It should wrap around the wrist twice. Tie a knot in each piece of suede a little over a third of the way up one side. Make a sample bracelet.

Wrap the cord around the person's wrist twice and cut. Tie a knot a little over a third of the way up one side. String your beads in the following order, using the *longer* side of your bracelet.

The first knot represents the day we were born.

Add the dark (black) bead. What makes our hearts dark and dirty? Who can name some sins? After we are born, do we have to be taught to sin? Who has sinned? Can God let sin into His perfect heaven?

Add the red bead. What did Jesus do for us? Did Jesus stay dead? Why is Jesus special? (He was God's Son.) Did Jesus ever sin? Why did Jesus die?

Add the clean (white) bead. How can we have our sins forgiven and washed away? Once we ask Jesus to be our Lord and Savior, will we ever sin again? When we do sin, does God still love us? What should we do? What does "Lord" mean? What does "Savior" mean? Once we ask Jesus to be our Lord and Savior, how should we live the rest of our lives?

Add the gold (yellow) bead. Revelation 21:21 says there is a street of gold in heaven. What else is in heaven? What is not in heaven? Because of our sins, we cannot get into heaven on our own. It is only when we ask Jesus to be our Lord and Savior and He takes away our sin that we can live with Him now and then someday in heaven.

Tie another knot to keep your beads snugly together. This knot represents when we die. If we ask Jesus to be our Lord and Savior, where do we go when we die?

Gather the two loose ends together so they are at the bottom, facing the same direction. Put both ends through your last bead at the same time. Tie knots in each of your loose ends. You may slide your sizing bead up and down to make your bracelet fit.

If you use a butterfly sizing bead, think about how a butterfly changes completely from a caterpillar to a butterfly. Jesus changes our life completely, too, when we ask Him to be our Lord and Savior. He takes away our sins, and we begin living for Him instead of ourselves. We become like a whole new person! We don't have to worry anymore, because God has everything under control. We don't have to be afraid, because God is always with us. As we learn more about Him, He helps us grow and change to become even more like Jesus.

Use your "tell me" bracelet to tell a friend about Jesus. If you have time, practice with a partner now.

Changed Heart Mobile

Younger and Older Kids: Jesus died for us.

Supplies Needed: White, black, yellow, and red construction paper; scissors; yarn or string; paper dinner plates or wire hangers; hole punch or tape

Advanced Preparation (optional): Cut four lengths of string per person, five if using paper plates. If using paper plates, cut them in half. Cut the paper into quarters. Cut out the shapes in advance or draw, print, or copy the following shapes on the correct colors: white heart, black heart, yellow circles, and red cross. Or find or make stencils of hearts, crosses, and circles to use.

If using paper plates, cut them in half. Tape a loop of string to the top of the curved edge or punch a hole in the top and tie a loop of string through the hole.

Cut the paper into quarters. You will need one quarter of each color per person.

Draw a circle on the gold (yellow) page, and cut it out. Punch a hole in the top to tie a length of string or tape it to the back. Attach it to the far left of the wire hanger or straight edge of the paper plate. Did you make a perfect circle? Did you know that it is very difficult to draw a circle perfectly without help? That reminds me of heaven. God's heaven is perfect, just like a perfect circle. Nothing bad can get in. What are some good and perfect things that will be in heaven? What are some bad things that will not be in heaven? We cannot get into heaven on our own.

Draw a heart on the dark (black) page, and cut it out. Punch a hole in the top to tie a length of string or tape it to the back. Leave a little space as you attach it next to the gold circle on the wire hanger or straight edge of the paper plate. What makes our hearts dark and dirty? Who can name some sins? Who has sinned? Can God let sin into His perfect heaven?

Draw a cross on the red page, and cut it out. Punch a hole in the top to tie a length of string or tape it to the back. Leave a little space as you attach it next to the dark heart on the wire hanger or straight edge of the paper plate. What did Jesus do for us? Did Jesus stay dead? Why is Jesus special? (He was God's Son.) Did Jesus ever sin? Why did Jesus die?

Draw a heart on the clean (white) page, and cut it out. Punch a hole in the top to tie a length of string or tape it to the back. Attach it to the far right of the wire hanger or straight edge of the paper plate. How can we have our sins forgiven and washed away? Once we ask Jesus to be our Lord and Savior, will we ever sin again? When we do sin, does God still love us? What should we do? What does "Lord" mean? What does "Savior" mean? Once we ask Jesus to be our Lord and Savior, how should we live the rest of our lives? What happens when we die?

Use your changed heart mobile to tell a friend about Jesus. If you have time, practice with a partner now.

The Jesus Bridge

Younger and Older Kids: Jesus died for us.

Supplies Needed: Masking tape, six to thirteen pieces of paper (enough to make a cross-shaped bridge across the room)

Use masking tape to mark off two sides of the room, leaving a gap in the middle and enough space for everyone to stand between the tape and the wall. One side is us, and the other is "heaven." Explain that we cannot make it to heaven on our own.

Put down the pieces of paper as a cross-shaped bridge, explaining that Jesus made the way for us to get to heaven. Read John 3:16 (NIV): "For God so loved the world that he gave his one and only Son, that whoever believes in him shall not perish but have eternal life."

Explain that each person has to decide to believe in Jesus on his or her own. You can't get in because someone else in your family believes. Have each person cross the bridge by himself or herself. Anyone who cannot cross the bridge alone in this game (e.g., mamas with babies or crawlers) will stay on the first side, reminding the group that not everyone gets into heaven. But everyone can cheer each time someone crosses over to the heaven side.

End the game praying those who do not know Jesus may come to know Him soon.

Week 6: Wrap It Up

Younger and Older Kids: Jesus died for us.

The first thing I did was place before you what was placed so emphatically before me: that the Messiah died for our sins, exactly as Scripture tells it; that he was buried; that he was raised from death on the third day, again exactly as Scripture says. (1 Corinthians 15:3–4 MSG)

If you already know Jesus as your Lord and Savior, the Bible tells us our job is to share that good news with others. If you still have questions or are not sure, God uses His Word to help us find those answers.

Where are you today? What step can you take this week to either share the good news with someone you know or look for the answers to some of your questions?

Week 6: Prayer Focus

Younger and Older Kids: Jesus died for us.

> Who foretold this long ago,
>   who declared it from the distant past?
> Was it not I, the LORD?
>   And there is no God apart from me,
> a righteous God and a Savior;
>   there is none but me.
> Turn to me and be saved.
>   all you ends of the earth;
> for I am God, and there is no other. (Isaiah 45:21–22 NIV)

The almighty God loves you. He had a plan to pay for your sin once and for all from the very beginning of time.

Are there any special praises or prayer requests this week?

End your prayer time asking God to continue to teach you more about Him.

Week 7: How Can a Family Follow God?

Sometimes I just have to be reminded that what I give to my children or what I do for my children is not as important as what I leave in them. Isn't it interesting how "stuff" can distract us from what is really valuable and how quickly we can get confused about what it means to be rich?

Reggie Joiner[19]

Main Point (Say this a lot today.)

> *Younger Kids:* Choose to serve God every day.
> *Older Kids:* Choose to serve God every day, *no matter what.*

Scripture

Samuel follows God, while Eli's sons do not—1 Samuel 1:27–28; 2:12–3:20.

Prepare Your Heart to Teach

Do other people know you are a Christian? How would they know if they didn't go to church with you?

> But someone might argue, 'Some people have faith, and others have good works.' My answer would be that you can't show me your faith if you don't do anything. But I will show you my faith by the good I do. You believe there is one God. That's good, but even the demons believe that! And they shake with fear. (James 2:18–19 ERV)

> The first step to a vibrant life-changing relationship with Christ is accepting Him as Lord and Savior, but it does not end there. Jesus is not content to simply be our life insurance policy or go-to guy in times of trouble. When God saved us from sin and death, He gave us new life in Jesus Christ, (2 Corinthians 5:17)

The life we now live should be for His glory. That means the things we do affect the family name of God. Will we give Christ honor as Christians or not? God sees all things, even those done in secret. He loves those who serve Him, even if no one else sees what they do. When we mess up (which we will), He still forgives us and helps us to continue to grow to be more like Christ (see 1 John 1:8–9; James 1:2–5).

I pray that the God of peace will give you every good thing you need so that you can do what he wants. God is the one who raised from death our Lord Jesus, the Great Shepherd of his sheep. He raised him because Jesus sacrificed his blood to begin the new agreement that never ends. I pray that God will work through Jesus Christ to do the things in us that please him. To him be glory forever. Amen. (Hebrews 13:20–21 ERV)

Week 7: Opening Activity (optional)

Do at least one of the following activities.

Chant It Out

Younger Kids: Choose to serve God every day.
Older Kids: Choose to serve God every day, *no matter what.*

Feel free to repeat previous Bible activities, or find more ideas at *www.MrMarksClassroom.com.*

Supplies Required: List or chart of the books of the Bible (Several Bibles open to the table of contents work as well.)

Use the following rhythm to create a beat: tap your legs (or the floor) twice, clap twice, repeat. On top of your beat, say all sixty-six books of the Bible in rhythm. Once you've got that, see if you can speed up your rhythm. How fast can you go? How slowly can you go? Can you switch every other book in a high voice and a low voice (GENESIS, Exodus, LEVITICUS, Numbers …)?

Stay in the Light

Younger Kids: Choose to serve God every day.
Older Kids: Choose to serve God every day, *no matter what.*

Supplies Needed: Flashlights (For younger groups, no more than one for every two to three people is recommended. For older groups, the fewer flashlights, the better. You know your group best.) The goal is to have some people who see well and others who can't see as well and must trust the one with the light.

Advanced Preparation: Clear the room of obstacles so you can play this game in the dark. Ensure there is at least one yellow item in the room.

Break learners into the same number of teams as you have flashlights (at least two to three per team; see note in "Supplies Needed"). Learners must *stay with their group* until the lights come back on. The game begins when the lights are turned out. Immediately after announcing the challenge, turn out the lights. The team that finds the most yellow items wins.

After playing for a while, turn the lights back on, and gather the troops to discuss. You may play again at the end if you still have time.

Was it always easy to see where you were going in this challenge? Why or why not?
Do you think it would be harder if there was no light at all in the room? Why or why not?
Have you ever been scared when you were in a dark place?

The Bible sometimes says that Jesus is like light shining in the darkness. Read John 8:12 (NIV): "When Jesus spoke again to the people, he said, 'I am the light of the world. Whoever follows me will never walk in darkness, but will have the light of life.'" We don't have to be scared when we follow Jesus. He shows us where we need to go and how to live. His love is so warm, He fills our lives with it like the light fills up this room. It's much better than a flashlight, isn't it? Jesus helps us to learn and grow like the sun helps the plants to grow. God wants us to learn about Him, pray and talk to Him, think about Him, and live for Him every day. That is what the Bible means when it says to walk in the light.

If you play this game again, switch who holds the flashlight, and use another color that symbolizes light or life (like white or green).

Music

> *Younger Kids:* Choose to serve God every day.
> *Older Kids:* Choose to serve God every day, *no matter what.*

Supplies Needed: A willingness to worship God through singing (Did I say sing well? Children just need someone to lead them. They are not critics.), CD and player (optional), computer with speakers (optional), DVD and player (optional), phone with music player (optional), instrument with player and music (optional)

Advanced Preparation: Choose the songs and how you will lead them.

Following you will find a variety of songs and styles. Please do not try to do them all. If you choose to do music, I recommend learning three to four songs over the course of the next seven weeks. Choose what works best for your group. For children, I would choose mostly fast songs and end with one slower, worshipful song. You decide what that means for your group. Feel free to change the order of the categories listed below. These songs may be found on *YouTube* and may be purchased on *iTunes* or CD. Some are also available on DVD.

God's Word Is the Source of Truth
"Jesus Loves Me" (There are lots of variations of this, for example, "Hey! Jesus Loves Me!" "Jesus Loves Me Rock")
There are several books of the Bible songs and raps. One puts the books to the tune of "Ten Little Indians."
"The Wise Man and the Foolish Man" ("The wise man built his house upon the rock …")
"Wonderful Words of Life," by Philip P. Bliss

Who God Is
"Better Is One Day," by Matt Redman or Kutless
"My God Is so Big"
"One Way," by Hillsong Kids
"Tell Me the Stories of Jesus," by Parker and Challinor

God Loves Me
"Amazing Grace" (or "My Chains Are Gone," by Chris Tomlin)
"He Knows My Name," by Maranatha Singers
"Get Down," by Audio Adrenaline
"Supernatural," by Hillsong Kids

Week 7: Bible Focus (optional[7])

Younger Kids: Choose to serve God every day.
Older Kids: Choose to serve God every day, *no matter what.*

Supplies Needed: Bible to teach from, yellow and black construction paper for each learner

Sometimes the Bible uses the word "Light" to talk about Jesus and following God. "Darkness" is sometimes used to talk about sin and those who do not follow God. Read John 3:19–20 (NIV): "This is the verdict: Light has come into the world, but people loved darkness instead of light because their deeds were evil. Everyone who does evil hates the light, and will not come into the light for fear that their deeds will be exposed."

Distribute one yellow and one black sheet of paper to each learner. Hold up the yellow sheet for light when someone in our Bible lesson today is doing something to honor God. Hold up the black sheet for dark when they are not.

Samuel's family loved and worshipped God (Light). Hannah wanted a baby very much, so she prayed for one (Light). God answered her prayer and gave her Samuel. When he was old enough, Hannah came back to the temple. Read 1 Samuel 1:27–28 (Light). Samuel's family went home, but he stayed and lived at the temple with the priest Eli and his family.

Read 1 Samuel 2:12 (Dark). Even though they were supposed to be priests, they were stealing from people and messing up their offerings to God. Read 1 Samuel 2:16–17. Was that very nice (Dark)? Read 1 Samuel 2:18–19 (Light).

Soon Eli heard what his sons were doing. Read 1 Samuel 2:23–25 (Dark).

Read 1 Samuel 2:26 (Light). How were Samuel and his family different from Eli's sons? Listen to what happened next.

One night Samuel thought Eli was calling him from his bed, but it wasn't Eli. The third time, Eli figured out it was God talking to Samuel. Read 1 Samuel 3:9–14. Was it good or bad that God spoke to Samuel (Light)? Was the news good or bad (Dark)?

Let's see what happened. Read 1 Samuel 3:15–18. Did Samuel follow God even though he was afraid (Light)? Did Eli trust God, even with bad news (Light)?

Read 1 Samuel 3:19–20. It's not always easy to live for God. Do you know someone who is not living for God? What are some things Samuel did that you can do?

- Obey God even when it's hard or you're afraid.
- Live for God even when others around you are not.
- Speak the truth in love. (Samuel still loved Eli. That is probably part of why he didn't want to tell him such bad news. Still, he loved him enough to not keep it from him.)

Week 7: Application Activities

Do at least one of the following activities.

On the Road Family Challenge Review

Younger Kids: Choose to serve God every day.
Older Kids: Choose to serve God every day, *no matter what.*

Supplies Needed: Paper or poster board, markers, frames or lamination (optional)

This world offers many distractions and opinions about how we should spend our time and where we should go to find the answers to our questions. Decide as a family to put God first and to turn to the Bible for answers. In family groups or as a large group, write the following verse on a paper or poster: "But as for me and my household, we will serve the LORD" (Joshua 24:15 NIV). (You can also look it up and do the whole verse.) Decorate it, and have everyone sign it. Hang it where all can see it.

Questions for each person:

What is one way you can serve God every day? (For young children, review ways to serve God before asking the question.)

What is something you do or see every day that can help you remember to serve God? (For younger children, ask something more specific, like, "How can you serve God every time it's time to eat?")

Set up a "secret code" to remind members of your family to keep God first (e.g., "How's your placement?" or, "Is your house straight?" or, "God first!"). Give every member of the family permission to ask anyone else how his or her spiritual walk is. Parents, don't be afraid to ask kids to pray for you, even if you don't give specifics. All you have to say is, "Mom just needs a little extra prayer today. God knows the details."

Ways to Serve God

Younger Kids: Choose to serve God every day.
Older Kids: Choose to serve God every day, *no matter what.*

Supplies Needed: None

> He has shown you, O mortal, what is good.
>> And what does the LORD require of you?
> To act justly and to love mercy
>> and to walk humbly with your God (Micah 6:8 NIV)

Act out the following situations, but problem solve together to find a way to serve God in each. (Be sure to act that out, too.) Feel free to add your own.

1. A classmate drops all his pencils at school. How can you serve God?
2. Your mom is folding the laundry when you come to ask her a question. How can you serve God?
3. Your brother is having a rotten day. How can you serve God?
4. You have extra food, and you know of someone who does not have enough. How can you serve God?
5. You just had the worst day ever. How can you serve God?
6. Your uncle who lives nearby is in the hospital. How can you serve God?
7. You're on vacation. How can you serve God?
8. You didn't make the team. How can you serve God?
9. The older lady who lives next door looks lonely. How can you serve God?
10. Someone made fun of you today. How can you serve God?
11. There is company coming to your house. How can you serve God?
12. You pet died today. How can you serve God?
13. You get to spend the night at a friend's house. How can you serve God?
14. Your church is having a special service or event for kids. How can you serve God?
15. It is test day at school (or evaluation day at work). How can you serve God?
16. You got invited to a party. How can you serve God?

An Ebenezer Reminder

Younger Kids: Choose to serve God every day.
Older Kids: Choose to serve God every day, *no matter what.*

Supplies Needed: Scissors, contact paper, tissue paper of various colors, yarn or string, tape, cardstock or construction paper, permanent markers, glue sticks (optional—white glue may pucker and run)

Advanced Preparation (optional): Precut one or two large oval frames from black, brown, or gray construction paper for each person, small squares of tissue paper in various colors, and a loop of yarn or ribbon, three to four inches long, for each person.

"Ebenezer" means stone of remembrance in Hebrew. At one time in Israel's history, they started listening to their neighbors and new friends who told them that God wasn't all He said He was. These friends trusted and followed other things when hard times and tough questions came in life. The people of Israel began to listen to what these friends said and forgot that

God is greater than anyone or anything else. God's Word is the place we should go for the answers to all life's questions. They forgot … until something really bad happened.

The ark of the covenant, which held the original Ten Commandments and other signs of the things God had done, was stolen by Philistines who were fighting and bullying Israel (1 Samuel 4). God punished the people who had it so severely that it wasn't long before they sent it back (1 Samuel 6). The prophet Samuel told the people, "If you return to the LORD with all your heart, remove the foreign gods and the Ashtaroth [idol] from among you and direct your hearts to the LORD and serve Him alone; and He will deliver you from the hand of the Philistines" (1 Samuel 7:3 NIV). The people did that, and Samuel prayed with them. Then they went into battle, and God gave them such a victory over the Philistines that they left Israel alone for a long time after that (1 Samuel 7).

To help the people remember what God did and their commitment to serve God, no matter what their friends and neighbors say, Samuel set up a big rock. "He named it Ebenezer, saying 'Thus far has the LORD helped us'" (1 Samuel 7:12). What does Ebenezer mean again?

Today you are going to make a colorful Ebenezer to hang in your window. It will remind you of all that God does for you and that He asks you to commit to follow Him, no matter what anyone else says.

Cut a large oval out of the center of a piece of cardstock or construction paper, and place it on the sticky side of a piece of contact paper. The sticky contact paper should still show through the oval.

Cut up (or tear) small pieces of tissue paper and put them inside the oval. If the layers get too thick, the light will not shine through.

Optional: Cover cardstock/construction paper with a thin layer of glue and a second piece of cardstock/construction paper with a matching oval hole cut from the center.

Before putting a second layer of contact paper on the top to seal, place a loop of yarn or string over the top with the loop free over the edge to hang the finished work.

Write on the outside with a permanent marker, "Serve God only" (1 Samuel 7:3).

Hang your beautiful Ebenezer in a window where you will see it often and remember the wonderful ways God has worked in your life.

Week 7: Wrap It Up

Younger Kids: Choose to serve God every day.
Older Kids: Choose to serve God every day, *no matter what.*

Jesus replied: "Love the Lord your God with all your heart and with all your soul and with all your mind." This is the first and greatest commandment. And the second is like it: "Love your neighbor as yourself." (Matthew 22:37–39 NIV)

We serve God when we show Him we love Him with all our heart, when we focus our mind on Him, and when we put our whole selves into living for Him. We also serve God when we love and serve other people, treating them the way we would like to be treated.

What is one specific example of something we can do to serve God?

Week 7: Prayer Focus

Younger Kids: Choose to serve God every day.
Older Kids: Choose to serve God every day, *no matter what.*

Attention, Israel! God, our God! God the one and only! Love God, your God, with your whole heart: love him with all that's in you, love him with all you've got! Write these commandments that I've given you today on your hearts. Get them inside of you and then get them inside your children. Talk about them wherever you are, sitting at home or walking in the street; talk about them from the time you get up in the morning to when you fall into bed at night. Tie them on your hands and foreheads as a reminder; inscribe them on the doorposts of your homes and on your city gates. (Deuteronomy 6:4–9 MSG)

God deserves and wants first place in our hearts and lives. He encourages us to do whatever it takes to remind ourselves and our families of that as we go through each day.

Are there any special praises or prayer requests this week?

End your prayer time telling God you love Him. Ask Him to show you how you can serve Him every day.

Part 2

Guide for Adult Groups

- *Review and Application:* Applies the week's main idea to today, mixing Bible study and discussion
- *Digging Deeper:* Asks a study focus question and digs into God's Word to find the answer
- *On the Road Challenge Debrief:* Discusses the weekly challenge (optional), used with an option above
- *Prayer Focus:* Take prayer requests and close with a prayer focus.

The "Guide for Multigenerational or Children's Groups" begins on page 1.

How Does This Work?

This small-group guide is designed for groups of two or more children or families. It could be used for a group of friends meeting regularly, breakfast groups, Bible study groups, Sunday school, a weekend family retreat, or any number of other occasions.

The small-group guide has two sections broken down to allow leaders to choose what works best within time constraints. This section includes the "Guide for Multigenerational and Children's Groups." The "Guide for Multigenerational and Children's Groups" begins on page 1.

Leaders are encouraged to be sure to choose at least one application activity, wrap up, and pray. The rest is optional, depending on your time and format. Little to zero leader prep time is required for all activities.

- *Prayer Focus*—Take prayer requests and close with a prayer linking back to that day's lesson.
- *Review and Application*—Applies the week's main idea to today, mixing Bible study and discussion.
- *Digging Deeper*—Asks a study focus question and digs into God's Word to find the answer.
- *On the Road Challenge Debrief* (optional)—Discusses the weekly challenge. Be sure to use this option along with one of the above. The "On the Road Family Challenge" is found in *The Answer Book: A Devotional for Busy Families.*★ These challenges may also be given the week before and used apart from this devotional.

  ★ This study is designed to partner with *The Answer Book: A Devotional for Busy Families*, but it may also stand alone. If you are using the *Devotional for Busy Families*, do the first week of the separate daily Bible study, gather your group, and then start with Week 1 in this guide.

Group members do not need to bring anything, though some may like to bring their Bibles.

Each week please be sure to include the following in your study.

- Encourage group members to *read* the Bible daily. This is not meant to be a guilt trip. When a day or more is missed, just pick up where you left off and keep going.
- Encourage group members to *apply* what they are learning with their families.
- *Pray* together. We cannot do any of this in our own strength.

If your situation allows, I encourage you to keep an open-door policy, welcoming new people at any time. This would apply even to those who might miss a week or two (or more).

Find a regular time for your group to meet, and let's get started!

Nancy Ruth
Parent Road Ministries

Teaching Tips

- *Provide a safe place.* Be sure to emphasize to your group members that what is said there should stay there. Without that kind of setting, you will not be able to build the trust and genuine sharing that fosters accountability and greatly aids spiritual growth.

- *Elevate the Prayer Focus.* If your group runs long, it is recommended that either the Prayer Focus open your time together or the discussion be cut short to still allow time for prayer at the end.

- *Feel free to change the order.* As the leader, you have freedom to arrange your class time to make it work best. Choose the activities you think will best present the lesson, and arrange them in the order to best suit. Keep in mind that different people learn in different ways, so try to provide a variety of activities over the next few weeks. They don't all have to be in the same lesson.

- *If you cancel a small-group meeting for any reason, do not cancel the at-home daily Bible study.* Strive to make Bible study a daily habit, no matter what life throws at you (see Psalm 1:1–3). See page 82 for suggestions on how to combine two weeks into one for the small group following your canceled meeting.

- *Stay positive.* Changing habits is hard. Encourage progress wherever you see it, no matter how small. Encourage learners to read the Bible, to pray, and to love God and other people. Just like God meets us where we are, loves us, and takes us from there, so we do that with other people as His followers.

- *Let people talk.* People feel valued when they are allowed to say what they have to say. This also fosters discussion. When people feel like they are cut off, they may begin to stop talking all together (unless they simply love to talk).

- *Avoid monopolies.* Do the same few people in your group answer all the questions and everyone else just sits there? Try naming a name before you ask a question. Allow the person time to think, but if he or she truly doesn't know, ask if the individual would like some help. Then either let the person choose a friend, or you can ask someone else. Make a point to draw out the quiet ones. You may be surprised what they contribute. Keep in mind that introverts often find it easier to begin by sharing ideas about things outside of themselves or about other (even hypothetical) people. Sharing their deeper thoughts, feelings, and personal stories, especially ones that involve hurt or shame, is a sign of great trust. It is not usually given lightly.

- *Don't be afraid of the silence.* Some groups take longer than others to respond to discussion questions, and that's okay. If you provide the answer too soon, you may be fostering a spirit of "wait for the teacher to provide the right answer." Try instead something like, "This is the discussion part," or ask if you need to repeat the question. You might also try going around the room for everyone to answer until your group gets the hang of discussion. But be aware some may be uncomfortable speaking in that setting.

- *Ask more questions.* Is your group reluctant to talk? While avoiding keeping the spotlight on anyone too long, ask follow-up questions to the short answers you get. Think of the 5 Ws and 1 H: In a show of hands, *who* else feels this way? *Who* else has experienced _____ (follow up on what was said or refer back to the original question)? *What* might that look like? Can you describe a time in your life *when* God reminded you of that very thing? *What* might be a situation *where* we might need to remember that? *Where* might we need to remember this? (After you get an answer to that question follow it with, *Why* that place? Then go back to the first and go again.) *Why* is this important? *How* do you know? What other questions can you think of? If you have trouble thinking of questions on the spot, make a list and keep it with your book.

- *If you have time, prepare Scriptures in advance.* Write or print the Bible references you will be using (or the whole verse) on separate slips of paper. As group members come, ask if they would be willing to read a verse. If so, give them one or more of your papers, have them look them up, and bookmark them to have them ready to read when needed. Be sure to provide extra Bibles. Keep in mind this takes longer if children are reading.

- *When choosing a version of Scripture to use as a "teaching Bible," consider your audience.* I usually recommend the *New International Version* (NIV) or *English Standard Version* (ESV) for children, but you may choose whichever version you like. Keep in mind that King James may require much more explanation on your part, since children are not as familiar with that form of English. One way to think of the different versions of the Bible is like the accelerated reader (AR) levels children are so familiar with from school. Children use the AR levels to choose books based on their reading ability. The higher the AR level, the harder the book. Different translations of the Bible serve a similar purpose. The original text was written in Greek, Hebrew, and Aramaic. These languages are very different from English in the way words and phrases are put together, not to mention what words mean. Some words have no exact word-to-word correlation. This makes it challenging to translate. For example, some of Paul's original Greek sentences, while grammatically correct for his day and language, would horrify English teachers today. His run-on sentences seem to last forever! Some English translations (like the *New American Standard Bible*) stay as close as they can to the original text and may seem harder to understand. Other English versions (like *The Message*) decide to take the meaning of the text and put it into easy to understand modern speech. Others (like the NIV) try to stay in the middle of the two extremes. The ESV is slightly easier to understand than the NIV.

- *Don't have a Bible?* Several good Bible apps are available, like the *YouBible*. You can also look up verses at www.biblegateway.com. Just type the reference as you see it into the search box. Be sure to scroll all the way down the page in case the verses appear in more than one frame. Many children may associate phones and the Internet primarily with games. It may be best to use a physical Bible with this age group.

- *New to using the Bible?* No problem! Scripture verses are given as book chapter:verse (i.e., Luke 3:2). Look up the book in the contents. Once you are in the right book, chapters are designated with either large numbers or headings, like "Chapter 1." Under each chapter number come smaller verse numbers, which restart with each chapter. Sometimes chapters continue into the next column or page. Deuteronomy 6:4–6, for example, would be the book of Deuteronomy (the fifth book of the Bible), the large number 6 (or the heading "Chapter 6"), and the smaller numbers 4, 5, and 6 within that chapter. Hint 1: Usually verse 1 is not numbered. Hint 2: Verses continue all the way until the next number, for example, "⁴Hear, O Israel: The Lord our God, the Lord is one. ⁵Love the Lord your God with all your heart and with all your soul and with all your strength. ⁶These commandments that I give you today are to be on your hearts."

How to Lead a Person to Christ

1) The first step is to *admit* (agree with God) *that you are a sinner.*

All we have to offer God that He[1] wants is our hearts broken over our sins. Tell Him you are sorry, and turn from your sins. Try not to do them anymore through God's forgiveness, mercy, and strength.

> Repent, then, and turn to God, so that your sins may be wiped out, that times of refreshing may come from the Lord, and that he may send the Messiah, who has been appointed for you—even Jesus. (Acts 3:19–20, NIV)

> The sacrifices of God are a broken spirit; A broken and a contrite heart, O God, You[2] will not despise. (Psalm 51:17 NASB; see also Ephesians 2:8–9; Isaiah 64:6)

A person ready to accept Christ as his or her Lord and Savior should understand the disconnect between God's perfect holiness and our sinful imperfections. Ask the following questions.

- What is heaven like? (See Revelation 21:1–22:7; Isaiah 11; 65:17–25.)
- Who lives in heaven? (See Acts 7:55–56; Isaiah 6:1–7; Revelation 4–5; 6:9–11; 7:4–17.)
- What is sin? (The wrong stuff we do: any thought, word, deed, or thing left undone that does not meet God's perfect standard. See Leviticus 11:45.)
- Can you name some sins? (See, for example, Romans 1:28–32.)
- Have you ever sinned? (Romans 3:23. God's perfection is the standard—Matthew 5:48; Leviticus 11:44.)

2) The second step is to *believe that Jesus is God's Son and that He died and rose again to pay for your sins.* Basically, Jesus is who He says He is, and He died and rose again to pay for our sins (1 Corinthians 15:3–4).

> that if you confess with your mouth Jesus as Lord, and believe in your heart that God raised Him from the dead, you will be saved; for with the heart a person believes, resulting in righteousness, and with the mouth he confesses, resulting in salvation. (Romans 10:9–10 NASB; see also 2 Corinthians 5:17)

A person ready to accept Christ as his or her Lord and Savior should understand who Jesus is and believe in Him. Ask the following questions.

- Who is Jesus? What did He do?
- Did Jesus ever sin? (Not even once; Hebrews 4:15; 2 Corinthians 5:21.)
- Why did Jesus die on the cross? Did He stay dead? (See 1 Corinthians 15:3–7.)
- Where is Jesus now? (Jesus is alive and seated at the right hand of God the Father in heaven. See Acts 1:9–11; 2:32–34. The Holy Spirit lives in the hearts of those who trust Him as their Lord and Savior. See John 14:16–18.)
- How can our sins be forgiven? (See Romans 10:9–10; John 1:12; 3:16.)
- What does "Savior" mean?
- Do you believe Jesus is who He says He is and that He did all of these things? (See Romans 10:9–10.)

3) The third step is to *commit to Jesus as your Lord and Savior.*

"Commit" means to decide to do something—decide firmly where nothing will change your mind. There will be times when this is difficult and times when it seems impossible, but God will help you (John 10:28–30; 1 Corinthians 10:13).

As Savior, Jesus took our penalty (punishment) for sin (Romans 5:8). Jesus takes our punishment, so our sins are forgiven and wiped clean forever (Psalm 103:12; Isaiah 1:18; 1 John 1:9; 1 Peter 3:18).

As Lord, Jesus is our life leader and worthy of our utmost respect and worship (Ephesians 1:20–22; Philippians 2:6–11).

A person ready to accept Christ as their Lord and Savior should understand this is a *lifetime commitment.* Ask the following questions.

- What does it meant to commit your life to Christ? (See Luke 9:23.)
- What does "Lord" mean?
- After we ask Jesus to be our Savior, will we ever sin again? (See Romans 7:18–20; 1 Corinthians 10:13.)
- What happens then? What do we do? (Turn from your sin, ask for forgiveness, and try not to do it again. God will help you; 1 Corinthians 10:13.)
- Are you ready to make this lifelong commitment to follow Jesus Christ as Lord and Savior, no matter what?

Let them pray and then pray for them, asking God to continue to teach them more about Him and draw them closer to Him.

How to Combine Two Weeks into One

There are several reasons small group may be canceled (holidays, weather emergencies, etc.). Here are some tips on how to adapt this curriculum in those situations.

1. Encourage the parents and members of your small group to continue with their at-home daily Bible study, *even when you are not meeting*. Our relationship with God does not stop when we go on vacation, but it takes conscious thought (and sometimes effort) to continue to make time with Him part of our day.

    If the members of your group don't actually finish every day while on vacation, that's fine. Celebrate the days you *did* do and keep going on together.

    > Blessed is the one
    > ... whose delight is in the law of the LORD,[3]
    >   and who meditates on his law day and night.
    > That person is like a tree planted by streams of water,
    >   which yields its fruit in season
    > and whose leaf does not wither—
    >   whatever they do prospers. (Psalm 1:1–3 NIV)

    Studies have shown that people will perform automated behaviors—like pulling out of a driveway or brushing teeth—the same way every single time, if they're in the same environment. But if they take a vacation, it's likely that the behavior will change.[4]

2. In the small-group meeting following your break, decide how to best use your time.

-   Skip the week you just did at home, and do the study of your current week.

    ○   For example,
        Last time you met you did Week 3.
        You did Week 4 in the at-home daily Bible study.
        When you meet again, you will discuss Week 5 as a small group.

-   Use the following guide. Feel free to adapt it as you see fit. Small-group members may find it helpful to bring their daily Bible studies.

Two Weeks in One Combination Option

Just get as far as you can in the amount of time you have. Be sure to leave time for the Prayer Focus at the end, or do that first.

Get Started

1. Welcome everyone back to small group.
2. "Blessed is the one ... whose delight is in the law of the LORD, and who meditates on his law day and night. That person is like a tree planted by streams of water, which yields its fruit in season and whose leaf does not wither—whatever they do prospers" (Psalm 1:1–3 NIV).

   Did you find it challenging to continue with your daily Bible study when we didn't meet? Why or why not?

3. What are some ways to help stay consistent in daily Bible study when life throws a curveball?

Discuss the Week Missed

- Remind the group of the topic of the week (found in the contents, page v). What was the main thing God taught you this week? What jumped out at you as you did your daily Bible study?

Discuss the Current Week

- Remind the group of the topic of the week (found in the contents, page 4). What was the main thing God taught you this week? What jumped out at you as you did your daily Bible study?

(If time) Discuss the On the Road Family Challenges[5]

1. How did your On the Road Family Challenges go the last two weeks?
2. Encourage those who missed this week's On the Road Family Challenge to take advantage of each week's family learning experiences.
3. Which one was more challenging and why?
4. What surprised you the most in these challenges?
5. What did you learn through these challenges?

Two Weeks in One Combination, Prayer Focus

Where can I go from your Spirit?
    Where can I flee from your presence?
If I go up to the heavens, you are there;
    if I make my bed in the depths, you are there.
If I rise on the wings of the dawn,
    if I settle on the far side of the sea,
even there your hand will guide me,
    your right hand will hold me fast.
If I say, "Surely the darkness will hide me
    and the light become night around me,"
even the darkness will not be dark to you;
    the night will shine like the day,
for darkness is as light to you. (Psalm 139:7–12 NIV)

God is with us and loves us wherever we go and whatever we do. We just have to choose to look for Him, listen, and follow Him. Are there any special prayer requests this week?

End your prayer time thanking God for bringing you safely back together. Ask Him to continue to draw you closer to Him.

Week 1: What Is a Worldview?

"Cows don't intend to get lost," the farmer explained,
"they just nibble their way to lostness!"[6]
… None of us intends to wander from the green pasture of God's voice!
None of us intends to have our souls wander onto the dull
and listless highway of the American Way.
First comes the tuft of education, then the tuft of marriage, then children, a new home,
and one day we wake up to discover that we have nibbled our way to lostness.

Michael Yaconelli[7]

Week 1: Prayer Focus

Doom to you! You pretend to have the inside track.
　　You shut God out and work behind the scenes,
Plotting the future as if you knew everything,
　　acting mysterious, never showing your hand.
You have everything backward!
　　You treat the potter as a lump of clay.
Does a book say to its author,
　　"He didn't write a word of me"?
Does a meal say to the woman who cooked it,
　　"She had nothing to do with this"? (Isaiah 29:15–16 MSG)

God's plan is not a secret. He wants us to seek and follow Him. He has promised to give us everything we need, for He knows those things better than we do. Are there any special prayer requests this week?

End your prayer time asking God for hearts willing to seek and follow Him, no matter what.

Week 1: Review and Application

Discussion Questions

1. Culture plays a major part in shaping our worldview. A culture is comprised of family, friends, music, media, food, language, faith practices (or philosophies), and other day-to-day habits, interactions, and ideas. What are some major influences in our culture today?

2. A worldview is a set of core beliefs that shape the way we view the world around us. It is shaped by the people, things, experiences, ideas, and habits that influence you the most. Other than God's Word, what are some of the people, experiences, or things that have had an impact on your life and the way you view the world?

Verses

All Scripture is God-breathed and is useful for teaching, rebuking, correcting and training in righteousness, so that the servant of God may be thoroughly equipped for every good work. (2 Timothy 3:16–17 NIV)

Your word is a lamp for my feet, a light on my path. (Psalm 119:105 NIV)

Discussion Question

- Read the following quote by Lindy Keffer.

Whatever happened to the *truth?!* In our world, the idea of ultimate truth—something that is true at all times in all places and has relevance for our lives—is about as extinct as the dinosaur. In fact, nearly three out of four Americans say there is no such thing as ultimate, or absolute, truth. And the numbers don't look much better among those who claim to follow Jesus.

In a society where ultimate truth is treated like a fairy tale, an outdated idea or even an insult to human intelligence, the motto of the day becomes, "WHATEVER!" Believe whatever you want. Do whatever seems best to you. Live for whatever brings you pleasure, as long as it doesn't hurt anyone. And of course, be tolerant. Don't try to tell anyone that their whatever is wrong.

But where does that leave us? If we have ultimate truth, it gives us both a way to explain the world around us and a basis for making decisions. Without it, we're alone.[8]

Is it hard or easy to allow the absolute truth of God's Word to guide your life? Why?

Verses

Love God, your God, with your whole heart: love him with all that's in you, love him with all you've got! Write these commandments that I've given you today on your hearts. Get them inside of you and then get them inside your children. Talk about them wherever you are, sitting at home or walking in the street; talk about them from the time you get up in the morning to when you fall into bed at night. Tie them on your hands and foreheads as a reminder; inscribe them on the doorposts of your homes and on your city gates. (Deuteronomy 6:5–9)

Discussion Question

- God wants to be part of everything we do. How might you incorporate Bible teaching into more of your everyday activities so children learn how to do this?

Verses

For the word of God is living and active. Sharper than any double-edged sword, it penetrates even to dividing soul and spirit, joints and marrow; it judges the thoughts and attitudes of the heart. Nothing in all creation is hidden from God's sight. Everything is uncovered and laid bare before the eyes of him to whom we must give account. (Hebrews 4:12–13 NIV)

Discussion Questions

1. Some of the things God's Word teaches are not easy. What has been some of the most challenging things God has taught you?
2. If you have one, what is your favorite promise from Scripture?

Week 1: Digging Deeper

Study Focus

A common adage in America today is "Follow your heart" or some variation thereof. Some spinoffs include, "Do what feels good," "Do what feels right to you," or "Whatever works for you." This idea is so pervasive that it can color our thinking in ways we don't even realize. Today we will study the following question.

- What does God's Word say about the heart and its trustworthiness?

Verses

> He who trusts in his own heart is a fool,
> But he who walks wisely will be delivered. (Proverbs 28:26 NASB)

> The fear of the LORD is the beginning of knowledge;
> Fools despise wisdom and instruction. (Proverbs 1:7 NASB)

Discussion Question

- Describe a time when "following your heart" either got you or a friend into trouble or into a less than ideal situation.

Verses

> Sin is the wrong stuff we do: any thought, word, deed, or thing left undone that does not meet God's perfect standard. (Leviticus 11:45)

> Who can say, "I have cleansed my heart,
> I am pure from my sin"? (Proverbs 20:9 NASB)

> For out of the heart come evil thoughts—murder, adultery, sexual immorality, theft, false testimony [lies], slander [insults and rumors]. (Matthew 15:19 NIV)

> The heart is deceitful above all things
>   and beyond cure.
>   Who can understand it?
> "I the LORD search the heart
>   and examine the mind,
> to reward each person according to their conduct,
>   according to what their deeds deserve." (Jeremiah 17:9–10 NIV)

Discussion Questions

1. What comes naturally out of the heart? Why is that?
2. Are children exempt from this?

Verses

Then the LORD God took the man and put him into the garden of Eden to cultivate it and keep it. The LORD God commanded the man, saying, "From any tree of the garden you may eat freely; but from the tree of the knowledge of good and evil you shall not eat, for in the day that you eat from it you will surely die." (Genesis 2:15–17 NASB)

When the woman saw that the tree was good for food, and that it was a delight to the eyes, and that the tree was desirable to make one wise, she took from its fruit and ate; and she gave also to her husband with her, and he ate. (Genesis 3:6 NASB)

Therefore, just as through one man sin entered into the world, and death through sin, and so death spread to all men, because all sinned. (Romans 5:12 NASB)

Discussion Question

- The consequences of Adam and Eve's sin are still seen today. How have you seen sin naturally flow from the hearts of your child(ren) or others you know?

Verses

Listen, my son, and be wise,
   and set your heart on the right path. (Proverbs 23:19 NIV)

Do not let your hearts be troubled; believe in God, believe also in Me. (Jesus speaking, John 14:1 NASB)

See to it, brothers and sisters [fellow believers in Christ], that none of you has a sinful, unbelieving heart that turns away from the living God. But encourage one another daily, as long as it is called "Today," so that none of you may be hardened by sin's deceitfulness. We have come to share in Christ, if indeed we hold our original conviction firmly to the very end. (Hebrews 3:12–14 NIV)

Discussion Questions

1. These are just a few of many verses where God tells us we can choose which way our hearts go. What are some ways we can choose set our hearts on a certain path?
2. How can we keep our hearts on the path of righteousness, on God's road of truth?

Verses

Search me, O God, and know my heart;
  Try me and know my anxious thoughts;
And see if there be any hurtful way in me,
  And lead me in the everlasting way. (Psalm 139:23–24 NASB)

Create in me a pure heart, O God,
  and renew a steadfast spirit within me. (Psalm 51:10 NASB)

Discussion Questions

1. How can we redirect our hearts to God's path?
2. What are some ways God may challenge what we always assumed to be true?
3. Something to think about: Would you be willing to consider the possibility that God may continue to challenge what you always assumed to be true, whether it be little or big things?

Week 1: On the Road Family Challenge Debrief (optional[5])

On the Road Family Challenge: Your mission is for everyone to make a list (or pictures) of things they see that are different from what God's Word teaches. If you have very young kids, be sure to include them. They may surprise you. Lists don't have to be perfect. Everyone should just do their best. On reporting day (Day 5), remind your family of the importance of knowing and studying God's Word to know what is true.

Encourage those who missed this week's On the Road Family Challenge to take advantage of each week's family learning experiences.

Discussion Questions

1. How did your On the Road Family Challenge go this week?
2. What were some of the things your family discovered? (If you haven't done it yet, what are some things you remember seeing this week?)
3. Were you able to counter each discovery with what God's Word says?
4. What challenges did you face in these or similar discussions?
5. James 1:5 (NIV) says, "If any of you lacks wisdom, he should ask God, who gives generously to all without finding fault, and it will be given to him." Have you found this to be the case or are there things you are still seeking wisdom to answer?

6. What types of sources surfaced (e.g., books, magazines, TV, school, Internet)?
7. What surprised you the most in this hunt?
8. What did you learn through this hunt?
9. Psalm 51:5–6 (NIV) says, "Surely I was sinful at birth, sinful from the time my mother conceived me. Surely you desire truth in the inner parts, you teach me wisdom in the inmost place." Who is the source of truth?
10. (If you have time) What are some ways we can teach our children that truth?

Week 2: Is There Only One Truth?

Only Scripture can claim to have absolute truth, for only
it comes straight to us from God Himself.
Knowledge that we gain from the use of the scientific
method still comes to us through people …
People are flawed, and, therefore, the results of their efforts,
no matter how careful and sincere they may be,
are also flawed. This is why so many scientific studies, even
in the realm of the natural or 'hard' sciences
are later contradicted by other studies.

John Babler, David Penley, and Mike Bizzell[9]

Week 2: Prayer Focus

But in your hearts revere Christ as Lord. Always be prepared to give an answer to everyone who asks you to give the reason for the hope that you have. But do this with gentleness and respect. (1 Peter 3:15 NIV)

At some point, someone will either ask us what we believe, why we believe it, or challenge what we believe. We may even wonder why the Bible says the things it does. God encourages us to look for the answers to our questions so we can know them for ourselves and be able to share them with others. Are there any praises or prayer requests this week?

End your prayer time thanking God for providing the answers to all your questions. Ask Him to continue to teach you more as you dig into His Word.

Week 2: Review and Application

Discussion Question

- What are some challenges you face or your family faces being Christian in a non-Christian world?

Verses

> People brought babies to Jesus, hoping he might touch them. When the disciples saw
> it, they shooed them off. Jesus called them back. "Let these children alone. Don't get
> between them and me. These children are the kingdom's pride and joy. Mark this:
> Unless you accept God's kingdom in the simplicity of a child, you'll never get in."
> (Luke 18:15–17, MSG)

One of the greatest privileges and toughest challenges parents and caregivers face is preparing their precious babies to go off on their own into the big, scary world as equipped and prepared adults, ready for the adventurous life God has for them. While Jesus never married or had physical children, He did take twelve uneducated, simple men and equipped them to boldly preach, change the world, start a revolutionary movement, and die for their faith[10]—all in three short years. Let's look at how He did it.

First Jesus went about the ministry God called Him to do. His public ministry began with His baptism. "The next day John saw Jesus coming toward him and said, 'Look, the Lamb of God, who takes away the sin of the world!'" (John 1:29 NIV).

"The next day John was there again with two of his disciples. When he saw Jesus passing by, he said,' Look, the Lamb of God!' When the two disciples heard him say this, they followed Jesus. Turning around, Jesus saw them following and asked, 'What do you want?' They said, 'Rabbi' (which means Teacher), 'where are you staying?' 'Come,' he replied, 'and you will see'" (John 1:35–39 NIV). Andrew was one of the two men who followed. He went to go get his brother Peter, who also started tagging along.

"The next day Jesus decided to leave for Galilee. Finding Philip, he said to him, 'Follow me'" (John 1:43 NIV). Then Philip brought Nathanael to meet Jesus, and he, too, began to follow.

Then exciting things began to happen. Jesus and His disciples went to a wedding they'd been invited to in Cana. The inexcusable happened, and the wine ran out. Jesus' mother came to Him, expecting a solution. She even told the servants to do whatever He asked. Even though Jesus demurred, He still worked a miracle, turning six large, stone water jars into the best wine of the party (John 2:1–10).

> This, the first of his miraculous signs, Jesus performed at Cana in Galilee. He thus
> revealed his glory, and his disciples put their faith in him. (John 2:11 NIV)

Nancy Ruth

Discussion Questions

1. So far, what has Jesus asked His disciples to do?
2. What has Jesus done?
3. What has been the result so far in the lives of the disciples?

Verses

Jesus continued to work miracles, answer His critics, and teach His disciples and the people, all the while keeping His disciples close, where they could see. He never lost track of doing the work He was called to do while He did so.

> After this, Jesus and his disciples went out into the Judean countryside, where he spent some time with them, and baptized. (John 3:22 NIV)

> When a Samaritan woman came to draw water, Jesus said to her, "Will you give me a drink?" (His disciples had gone into town to buy food.) … The woman said, "I know that Messiah" (called Christ) "is coming. When he comes, he will explain everything to us." Then Jesus declared, "I who speak to you am he." Just then his disciples returned and were surprised to find him talking with a woman. But no one asked, "What do you want?" or "Why are you talking with her?" (John 4:7–8, 25–27 NIV)

Discussion Questions

1. What has Jesus asked His disciples to do?
2. What has Jesus done?
3. What has been the result so far in the lives of the disciples?

Verses

> When Jesus looked up and saw a great crowd coming toward him, he said to Philip, "Where shall we buy bread for these people to eat?" He asked this only to test him, for he already had in mind what he was going to do. Philip answered him, "It would take more than half a year's wages to buy enough bread for each one to have a bite!" Another of his disciples, Andrew, Simon Peter's brother, spoke up, "Here is a boy with five small barley loaves and two small fish, but how far will they go among so many?" Jesus said, "Have the people sit down." There was plenty of grass in that place, and they sat down (about five thousand men were there). Jesus then took the loaves, gave thanks, and distributed to those who were seated as much as they wanted. He did the same with the fish. (John 6:5–11 NIV)

Discussion Questions

1. What has Jesus begun to ask His disciples to do?
2. Do they always get things "just right"?
3. What does Jesus do?
4. What has been the result so far in the lives of the disciples?

Verses

When Jesus had called the Twelve together, he gave them power and authority to drive out all demons and to cure diseases, and he sent them out to proclaim the kingdom of God and to heal the sick. He told them: "Take nothing for the journey— no staff, no bag, no bread, no money, no extra shirt. Whatever house you enter, stay there until you leave that town. If people do not welcome you, leave their town and shake the dust off your feet as a testimony against them." So they set out and went from village to village, proclaiming the good news and healing people everywhere … When the apostles returned, they reported to Jesus what they had done. Then he took them with him and they withdrew by themselves to a town called Bethsaida, but the crowds learned about it and followed him. He welcomed them and spoke to them about the kingdom of God, and healed those who needed healing. (Luke 9:1–6, 10–11 NIV)

Shortly before dawn Jesus went out to them, walking on the lake. When the disciples saw him walking on the lake, they were terrified. "It's a ghost," they said, and cried out in fear. But Jesus immediately said to them: "Take courage! It is I. Don't be afraid." "Lord, if it's you," Peter replied, "tell me to come to you on the water." "Come," he said. Then Peter got down out of the boat, walked on the water and came toward Jesus. But when he saw the wind, he was afraid and, beginning to sink, cried out, "Lord, save me!" Immediately Jesus reached out his hand and caught him. "You of little faith," he said, "why did you doubt?" And when they climbed into the boat, the wind died down. (Matthew 14:25–32 NIV)

On hearing it, many of his disciples said, "This is a hard teaching. Who can accept it?" Aware that his disciples were grumbling about this, Jesus said to them, "Does this offend you? Then what if you see the Son of Man ascend to where he was before! The Spirit gives life; the flesh counts for nothing. The words I have spoken to you—they are full of the Spirit and life. Yet there are some of you who do not believe." For Jesus had known from the beginning which of them did not believe and who would betray him. He went on to say, "This is why I told you that no one can come to me unless the Father has enabled them." From this time many of his disciples turned back and no longer followed him. "You do not want to leave too, do you?" Jesus asked the Twelve. Simon Peter answered him, "Lord, to whom shall we go? You have the words of eternal life. We have come to believe and to know that you are the Holy One of God." Then Jesus replied, "Have I not chosen you, the Twelve? Yet one of you is a devil!" (He meant Judas, the son of Simon Iscariot, who, though one of the Twelve, was later to betray him). (John 6:60–71 NIV)

Discussion Questions

1. What has Jesus begun to ask His disciples to do?
2. What happens when they are finished?
3. What does Jesus do?
4. What has been the result in the lives of the disciples?

Verses

"But you will receive power when the Holy Spirit comes on you; and you will be my witnesses in Jerusalem, and in all Judea and Samaria, and to the ends of the earth." After he said this, he was taken up before their very eyes, and a cloud hid him from their sight. (Acts 1:8–9 NIV)

With great power the apostles continued to testify to the resurrection of the Lord Jesus. And God's grace was so powerfully at work in them all. (Acts 4:33 NIV)

Discussion Questions

1. What has Jesus asked His disciples to do?
2. What did Jesus do?
3. What has been the result in the lives of the disciples?
4. How could the way Jesus worked with His disciples apply to how children are raised in the faith?

Verses

We have much to say about this, but it is hard to make it clear to you because you no longer try to understand. In fact, though by this time you ought to be teachers, you need someone to teach you the elementary truths of God's word all over again. You need milk, not solid food! Anyone who lives on milk, being still an infant, is not acquainted with the teaching about righteousness. (Hebrews 5:11–13 NIV)

Discussion Question

- Is there a biblical age limit on what children can do for the Lord?

Week 2: Digging Deeper

Study Focus

Statistician Peter Stoner said that the odds of one person (like Jesus) to have fulfilled just eight prophecies in their lifetime is 1 in 100,000,000,000,000,000.[11] Jesus fulfilled more than one hundred Old Testament prophecies.

Today we will study the following question.

- What are some Old Testament prophecies Jesus fulfilled?

Verses

But in the same night the word of the LORD came to Nathan, saying, "Go and say to My servant David," Thus says the LORD ... "When your days are complete and you lie down with your fathers, I will raise up your descendant after you, who will come forth from you, and I will establish his kingdom. He shall build a house for My name, and I will establish the throne of his kingdom forever." (2 Samuel 7:4–5, 12–13 NASB)

"Behold, the days are coming," declares the LORD,
"When I will raise up for David a righteous Branch;
And He will reign as king and act wisely
And do justice and righteousness in the land." (Jeremiah 23:5 NASB)

But they shall serve the LORD their God and David their king, whom I will raise up for them. (Jeremiah 30:9 NASB)

The record of the genealogy of Jesus the Messiah, the son of David, the son of Abraham. (Matthew 1:1 NASB)

The angel also told Mary, "He will be great and will be called the Son of the Most High; and the Lord God will give Him the throne of His father David." (Luke 1:32 NASB)

After He [God] had removed him [Saul], He raised up David to be their king, concerning whom He also testified and said, "I have found David the son of Jesse, a man after My heart, who will do all My will." From the descendants of this man, according to promise, God has brought to Israel a Savior, Jesus. (Acts 13:22–23 NASB)

Discussion Questions

1. What was the prophecy?
2. How was it fulfilled?
3. King David reigned from 1000 to 960 BC. Jesus was born 7 or 6 BC.[12] How long did the nation of Israel have to wait for this prophecy to be fulfilled?

Verses

But as for you, Bethlehem Ephrathah,
Too little to be among the clans of Judah,
From you One will go forth for Me to be ruler in Israel.
His goings forth are from long ago,
From the days of eternity."
Therefore He will give them up until the time
When she who is in labor has borne a child.
Then the remainder of His brethren
Will return to the sons of Israel.
And He will arise and shepherd His flock
In the strength of the LORD,
In the majesty of the name of the LORD His God.
And they will remain,
Because at that time He will be great
To the ends of the earth.
This One will be our peace.
When the Assyrian invades our land,
When he tramples on our citadels,
Then we will raise against him
Seven shepherds and eight leaders of men (Micah 5:2–5 NASB)

Now after Jesus was born in Bethlehem of Judea in the days of Herod the king, magi from the east arrived in Jerusalem, saying, "Where is He who has been born King of the Jews? For we saw His star in the east and have come to worship Him." When Herod the king heard this, he was troubled, and all Jerusalem with him. Gathering together all the chief priests and scribes of the people, he inquired of them where the

Messiah was to be born. They said to him, "In Bethlehem of Judea; for this is what
has been written by the prophet:

'And you, Bethlehem, land of Judah,

Are by no means least among the leaders of Judah;

For out of you shall come forth a Ruler

Who will shepherd My people Israel.'" (Matthew 2:1–6 NASB)

Discussion Questions

1. What was the prophecy?
2. How was it fulfilled?
3. The book of Micah was written "in the days of Jotham, Ahaz, and Hezekiah, kings of
    Judah" (Micah 1:1 NIV), about 750–687 BC.[13] Jesus was born 7 or 6 BC. How long
    did the nation of Israel have to wait for this prophecy to be fulfilled?

Verses

Rejoice greatly, O daughter of Zion!

Shout in triumph, O daughter of Jerusalem!

Behold, your king is coming to you;

He is just and endowed with salvation,

Humble, and mounted on a donkey,

Even on a colt, the foal of a donkey. (Zechariah 9:9 NASB)

As they approached Jerusalem, at Bethphage and Bethany, near the Mount of Olives,
He sent two of His disciples, and said to them, "Go into the village opposite you,
and immediately as you enter it, you will find a colt tied there, on which no one
yet has ever sat; untie it and bring it here. If anyone says to you, 'Why are you
doing this?' you say, 'The Lord has need of it'; and immediately he will send it
back here." They went away and found a colt tied at the door, outside in the street;
and they untied it. Some of the bystanders were saying to them, 'What are you
doing, untying the colt?' They spoke to them just as Jesus had told them, and they
gave them permission. They brought the colt to Jesus and put their coats on it;
and He sat on it. And many spread their coats in the road, and others spread leafy
branches which they had cut from the fields. Those who went in front and those
who followed were shouting:

"Hosanna!

Blessed is He who comes in the name of the Lord;

Blessed is the coming kingdom of our father David;

Hosanna in the highest!" (Mark 11:1–10, NASB)

Discussion Questions

1. What was the prophecy?
2. How was it fulfilled?
3. The prophecies in the book of Zechariah was most likely given, collected, and written between the years 520 and 475 BC.[14] This happened the week Jesus died, in AD 30.[15] How long did the nation of Israel have to wait for this prophecy to be fulfilled?

Verses

> For dogs have surrounded me;
> A band of evildoers has encompassed me;
> They pierced my hands and my feet. (Psalm 22:16 NASB)

> I will pour out on the house of David and on the inhabitants of Jerusalem, the Spirit of grace and of supplication, so that they will look on Me whom they have pierced; and they will mourn for Him, as one mourns for an only son, and they will weep bitterly over Him like the bitter weeping over a firstborn. (Zechariah 12:10 NASB)

> And when they had crucified Him, they divided up His garments among themselves by casting lots. (Matthew 27:35 NASB)

> So the other disciples were saying to him, "We have seen the Lord!" But he said to them, "Unless I see in His hands the imprint of the nails, and put my finger into the place of the nails, and put my hand into His side, I will not believe."

> After eight days His disciples were again inside, and Thomas with them. Jesus came, the doors having been shut, and stood in their midst and said, "Peace be with you." Then He said to Thomas, "Reach here with your finger, and see My hands; and reach here your hand and put it into My side; and do not be unbelieving, but believing." Thomas answered and said to Him, "My Lord and my God!" Jesus said to him, "Because you have seen Me, have you believed? Blessed are they who did not see, and yet believed." (John 20:25–29 NASB)

Discussion Questions

1. What was the prophecy?
2. Psalm 22 was written by David (Psalm 22:1, see the small print before "My God") who reigned between 1000 BC and 960 BC. The prophecies in the book of Zechariah was most likely given, collected, and written between the years 520 and 475 BC.

Crucifixion was used as a means of capital punishment by the Persians, Seleucids, Carthaginians, and Romans from about the sixth century BC to the fourth century AD.[16] Jesus was crucified in AD 30. How was this prophecy fulfilled?

Verses

> I have set the LORD continually before me;
> Because He is at my right hand, I will not be shaken.
> Therefore my heart is glad and my glory rejoices;
> My flesh also will dwell securely.
> For You will not abandon my soul to Sheol;
> Nor will You allow Your Holy One to undergo decay.
> You will make known to me the path of life;
> In Your presence is fullness of joy;
> In Your right hand there are pleasures forever. (Psalm 16:8–11 NASB)

"He is not here, but He has risen. Remember how He spoke to you while He was still in Galilee, saying that the Son of Man must be delivered into the hands of sinful men, and be crucified, and the third day rise again." And they remembered His words. (Luke 24:6–8 NASB)

Remember Jesus Christ, risen from the dead, descendant of David, according to my gospel. (2 Timothy 2:8 NASB)

Discussion Questions

1. What was the prophecy?
2. Psalm 16 was written by David (Psalm 16:1, see the small print before "My God") who reigned between 1000 BC and 960 BC. Jesus was crucified in AD 30. How was this prophecy fulfilled?

Week 2: On the Road Family Challenge Debrief (optional[5])

On the Road Family Challenge: Grab a blindfold and a variety of objects (stuffed animal, pot, hat, book, mug, sports equipment, a closed purse, one shoe, a puzzle piece, a marker, etc.). Only let one person see the objects in question. Hide them in a suitcase, under the table, in the kitchen cabinet, or wherever you like. Take turns blindfolding each other. The person who knows what the objects are should place one object into the hands of the blindfolded person. That person should use his or her hands, ears, nose, and possibly tongue to describe as much as possible about the object he or she is holding to the rest of the family (which can see it, but can't say anything). Try to describe how the object looks and its color, too. If you don't know, guess. When finished, take off the blindfold and start again with someone else.

Encourage those who missed this week's On the Road Family Challenge to take advantage of each week's family learning experiences.

Discussion Questions

1. How did your On the Road Family Challenge go this week?
2. What surprised you the most in this challenge?
3. What did you learn through this challenge or this week in Bible study?
4. What are some things you wish you knew or understood about God?
5. What are some things that amaze you about God?
6. We do the best we can for our families, but there is only so much time in the day, and we are not superheroes. In caring for your family, are there times things slip through the cracks?
7. God holds time in His hands (2 Peter 3:8) and is in all places at all times (Jeremiah 23:24). He knows everything (Proverbs 15:3). Do you find that comforting or scary? Why?
8. Human beings tend to like what is familiar. The unknown can be scary and difficult to handle. As a result, some people consciously or unconsciously put God into a box of their own creation, one that stays within the parameters of their understanding.

> But will God really dwell on earth with humans? The heavens, even the highest heavens, cannot contain you. How much less this temple I have built! Yet, Lord my God, give attention to your servant's prayer and his plea for mercy. Hear the cry and the prayer that your servant is praying in your presence. (2 Chronicles 6:18–19 NIV)

God is so much greater than we can comprehend, yet He knows everything about us and cares for us.

What are some ways you've seen people try to limit who God is?

9. (If you have time) What are some ways we can teach our children about God as He really revealed Himself in His Word?

Week 3: Why Spend Time with God?

This is what God wants most from you: a relationship!
It's the most astounding truth in the universe—
that our Creator wants to fellowship with us.
God made you to love you, and he longs for you to love him back.

Rick Warren[17]

Week 3: Prayer Focus

"You're blessed when you stay on course,
    walking steadily on the road revealed by God.
You're blessed when you follow his directions,
    doing your best to find him. (Psalm 119:1–2 MSG)

God wants us to rest in Him and in His Word. He holds us in His hands. Are there any special prayer requests this week?

End your prayer time asking God to give you a fresh hunger for His Word.

Week 3: Review and Application

Verses

When David was a boy, he was chosen and anointed king of Israel by a prophet of the Lord. When Samuel arrived at David's house, he looked over all the older brothers, all very promising young men. "But the LORD said to Samuel, 'Do not consider his appearance or his height, for I have rejected him. The LORD does not look at the things man looks at. Man looks at the outward appearance, but he LORD looks at the heart'" (1 Samuel 16:7 NIV). Finally, Samuel ran out of brothers and learned David was out tending sheep. He had the boy sent for and held the meal until he came. Samuel then anointed David the next king of Israel (1 Samuel 16:1–13).

Discussion Question

- How do you think David expected his life to turn out when Samuel left his father's tent that day? Even if you know the rest of this story, use your imaginations here, and put yourself in David's shoes at that age.

Verses

David was often brought to the royal court after that for his harp playing skills. He was handsome, strong, had a good reputation, was known as a man of God, and his music could calm the king when the evil spirit tormented him (1 Samuel 16:14–23). David's first military victory is a story known to many (1 Samuel 17).

Read 1 Samuel 17:4–7 (MSG).

A giant nearly ten feet tall stepped out from the Philistine line into the open, Goliath from Gath. He had a bronze helmet on his head and was dressed in armor—126 pounds of it! He wore bronze shin guards and carried a bronze sword. His spear was like a fence rail—the spear tip alone weighed over fifteen pounds. His shield bearer walked ahead of him.

Read 1 Samuel 17:11 (MSG).

When Saul and his troops heard the Philistine's challenge, they were terrified and lost all hope.

According the challenge Goliath issued, if a champion of Israel defeated him, they would claim the victory for the entire army, and the Philistines would be their slaves. However, if Goliath won, the tables would be turned. Day after day the giant issued his challenge, but no one came to meet him, even though the king offered a great reward.

Discussion Question

- What kinds of challenges have you faced that cause you to be terrified or lose all hope?

Verses

One day, little David came with a care package from his dad to his brothers in the army. He heard the challenge and asked several people why no one went to meet the foreigner. Finally, he was brought to the king.

Read 1 Samuel 17:32–37 (MSG).

> "Master," said David, "don't give up hope. I'm ready to go and fight this Philistine."
>
> Saul answered David, "You can't go and fight this Philistine. You're too young and inexperienced—and he's been at this fighting business since before you were born."
>
> David said, "I've been a shepherd, tending sheep for my father. Whenever a lion or bear came and took a lamb from the flock, I'd go after it, knock it down, and rescue the lamb. If it turned on me, I'd grab it by the throat, wring its neck, and kill it. Lion or bear, it made no difference—I killed it. And I'll do the same to this Philistine pig who is taunting the troops of God-Alive. God, who delivered me from the teeth of the lion and the claws of the bear, will deliver me from this Philistine."
>
> Saul said, "Go. And God help you!"

God gave the victory to David and the Israelites that day. He killed the proud giant with just a sling and a river stone.

Discussion Questions

1. When you approach an impossible task, do you tend to have an attitude more similar to the Israelites or to David? Why do you think that is?
2. Do you think your life might change if you approached at least one seemingly impossible task with the attitude of David? Why or why not?

Verses

> David's victory brought him to live in the royal court and the public eye. He also became very close friends with Jonathan, the king's son (1 Samuel 18:1–4). Read 1 Samuel 18:5–9 (NIV).
>
> Whatever mission Saul sent him on, David was so successful that Saul gave him a high rank in the army. This pleased all the troops, and Saul's officers as well.
>
> When the men were returning home after David had killed the Philistine, the women came out from all the towns of Israel to meet King Saul with singing and dancing, with joyful songs and with timbrels and lyres. As they danced, they sang:
>
> "Saul has slain his thousands,
>   and David his tens of thousands."
>
> Saul was very angry; this refrain displeased him greatly. "They have credited David with tens of thousands," he thought, "but me with only thousands. What more can he get but the kingdom?" And from that time on Saul kept a close eye on David.

David went on the run when the king tried multiple times to kill him (1 Samuel 18:6–19:17). Though he had more than one chance to kill the king in return, David refused, trusting in the Lord and His perfect timing (1 Samuel 24; 26). Once King Saul finally died at another's hands in battle, David still lived in contention for years with Saul's son before he received the unified kingdom promised to him as a boy (2 Samuel 3:1; 5:1–5). Even then, his reign was not always sunshine and roses.

Discussion Questions

1. How do you tend to react when things don't go the way you expect?
2. Where do you tend to turn for strength and comfort when you get discouraged, overwhelmed, or attacked by others?

Verses

During his time on the run and rule as king, David kept up his music and wrote many psalms which are really songs. Read Psalm 9:9–10 (NIV):

> The LORD is a refuge for the oppressed,
> a stronghold in times of trouble.
> Those who know your name trust in you,
> for you, LORD, have never forsaken those who seek you.

Discussion Questions

1. The Lord never forsakes those who seek Him. What are some ways we can seek the Lord?
2. What are some ways we can incorporate seeking the Lord into our daily lives?

Week 3: Digging Deeper

Study Focus

God gave the people of Israel His Word directly, but because they neglected it, they forgot what it said and drifted away from God. Today we will study the following two questions.

1. What happens when we neglect God's Word?
2. Is the situation reversible?

Verses

The book of Judges begins right after Joshua with the death of that great leader and the land in the process of being conquered. Read some of Joshua's parting words in Joshua 24:14–15, 19–20 (NASB).

Now, therefore, fear the LORD and serve Him in sincerity and truth; and put away the gods which your fathers served beyond the River and in Egypt, and serve the LORD. If it is disagreeable in your sight to serve the LORD, choose for yourselves today whom you will serve: whether the gods which your fathers served which were beyond the River, or the gods of the Amorites in whose land you are living; but as for me and my house, we will serve the LORD …

Then Joshua said to the people, "You will not be able to serve the LORD, for He is a holy God. He is a jealous God; He will not forgive your transgression or your sins. If you forsake the LORD and serve foreign gods, then He will turn and do you harm and consume you after He has done good to you."

Discussion Questions

1. Do you have someone in your life who encourages you to stay grounded in God's Word? If so, who?
2. In what ways would worshipping and serving God as a family/household be helpful?

Verses

The book of Judges goes on to demonstrate a cycle that repeats through the following generations (i.e., Judges 3:7–11, 12–30).

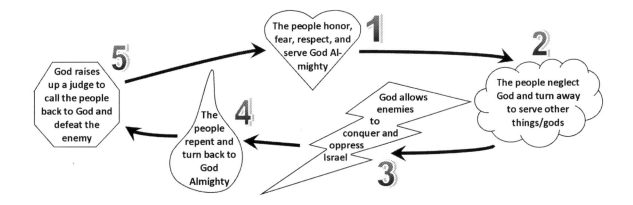

1. The people honor, fear, respect, and serve God Almighty.
2. The people neglect God and turn away to serve other things/gods.
3. God allows enemies to conquer and oppress Israel.
4. The people repent and turn back to God.
5. God raises up a judge to call the people back to God and defeat the enemy.

Read the conclusion of Judges in 21:25 (NASB).

> In those days there was no king in Israel; everyone did what was right in his own eyes.

The people had come a long way from their promise to serve God as Joshua had.

Discussion Question

- How do you think the people of Israel went from following God and trusting Him in the wilderness and battle to neglecting His leadership and doing their own thing?

Verses

> Israel next asked Samuel, the last judge, to anoint them a king like the nations around them. In doing so, they rejected God's leadership, choosing to follow the example of the other nations instead and trust in a human leader to save them from any trouble (1 Samuel 8).

Discussion Question

- Are there times you find yourself waiting for someone other than God to solve your problems? (If only so-and-so would [fill in the blank] …) Does it help?

Verses

Saul was the first king of Israel, but he was a king like the other nations and did not do what was pleasing to the Lord (1 Samuel 8:20; 15:22–23, 26). Because of this, God rejected him. Read what happened next in Acts 13:22 (NASB).

> After He had removed him, He raised up David to be their king, concerning whom He also testified and said, "I have found David the son of Jesse, a man after My heart, who will do all My will."

The kingdom prospered under David, and God continued that blessing under Solomon, the next king, because of David (2 Samuel 7:8–16). However, Solomon was influenced by the pagan ideas worship that his many wives introduced. He was not faithful to the Lord like his father David (Nehemiah 13:26). In fact, the kingdom split in half after King Solomon died because of his sin (1 Kings 11:29–12:24).

Jeroboam, the first king of northern Israel, drove out the priests of the Lord and set up idol worship in order to keep people from returning to Jerusalem (in the southern kingdom of Judah) for worship (1 Kings 12:25–33; 2 Chronicles 11:14–17). Although there were some good kings sprinkled in the mix who brought reform, each generation generally got progressively worse in their neglect of God and His Word (1 Kings 12–2 Kings 25; 2 Chronicles 10–36).

Throughout this time, the prophets warned the people of the consequences of their actions.

> The LORD sends a message against Jacob,
> And it falls on Israel …
> Yet the people do not turn back to Him who struck them,
> Nor do they seek the LORD of hosts.
> So the LORD cuts off head and tail from Israel,
> Both palm branch and bulrush in a single day.
> The head is the elder and honorable man,
> And the prophet who teaches falsehood is the tail.
> For those who guide this people are leading them astray;
> And those who are guided by them are brought to confusion. (Isaiah 9:8, 13–16, NASB)

> Now in that day the remnant of Israel, and those of the house of Jacob who have escaped, will never again rely on the one who struck them, but will truly rely on the LORD, the Holy One of Israel.

> A remnant will return, the remnant of Jacob, to the mighty God. (Isaiah 10:20–21 NASB)

Discussion Questions

- Have there been times in your life when something or someone reminded you not to neglect the important things in life? What happened? Did you listen?

Verses

> Jesus said, "I am the true vine, and My Father is the vinedresser. Every branch in Me that does not bear fruit, He takes away; and every branch that bears fruit, He prunes

it so that it may bear more fruit. You are already clean because of the word which I have spoken to you. Abide in Me, and I in you. As the branch cannot bear fruit of itself unless it abides in the vine, so neither can you unless you abide in Me" (John 15:1–4 NASB).

Discussion Questions

1. How can we abide in Christ?
2. How do you think regular time in God's Word might change how you approach your day?
3. What are some ways you might be able to have some alone time with God? (See sidebar.)
4. When are some ways you might be able to make that happen?

Week 3: On the Road Family Challenge Debrief (optional[5])

On the Road Family Challenge: This week, plan one day to gather the family for a "praise fest." Set a timer for thirty seconds, and see how many things you can name to be thankful for about God and things He's done for you or given to you. Now you're on a roll, set the timer and go again! If you need to, narrow the topic, but keep it to praise.

Encourage those who missed this week's On the Road Family Challenge to take advantage of each week's family learning experiences.

Discussion Questions

1. How did your On the Road Family Challenge go this week?
2. What surprised you the most in this hunt?
3. Is it hard or easy to think of things for which to praise God?
4. Was it easier the second and third time you tried it?
5. What did you learn through this hunt?
6. Are you in the habit of praising God daily?
7. Is it hard or easy to look for things for which to be thankful in the midst of our everyday lives? Why do you think that is?
8. What are some things in your life that distract you from being thankful or tend to foster discouragement?
9. Hebrews 4:14–16 (MSG) says, "Now that we know what we have—Jesus, this great High Priest with ready access to God—let's not let it slip through our fingers. We don't have a priest who is out of touch with our reality. He's been through weakness

and testing, experienced it all—all but the sin. So let's walk right up to him and get what he is so ready to give. Take the mercy, accept the help." Jesus regularly made time to be alone with the Father for strength. Do you find that hard or easy to do? Why?

10. Psalm 106:1 (NIV) says, "Praise the LORD. Give thanks to the LORD, for he is good; his love endures forever." How do you think we can foster a more thankful spirit every day of the week?

11. (If you have time) What are some ways we can teach our children to remember to thank God for who He is and what He does for us?

Week 4: Who Are the People God Can Use?

Don't let what's wrong with you keep you from worshiping what's right with God.

Mark Batterson[18]

Week 4: Prayer Focus

Join with others in following my example, brothers and take note of those who live according to the pattern we gave you. (Philippians 3:17 NIV)

The Bible gave us lots of good examples of men and women who followed God in all they did. Are there any special praises or prayer requests this week?

End your prayer time asking God to help you be a good example to other believers.

Week 4: Review and Application

Discussion Question

- Who are some of your heroes in the Bible? What makes you look up to them?

Sometimes, the great works of people we consider "giants" in the faith overshadow their humble beginnings and ongoing struggles. Today we'll look at some passages that remind us that the men and women God shaped into pillars of the faith were ordinary men and women like us.

Verses

When God told Abraham (then called Abram) to leave home, He told him,

> Go from your country, your people and your father's household to the land I will show you.
> I will make you into a great nation,
>   and I will bless you;

> I will make your name great,
>   and you will be a blessing.
> I will bless those who bless you,
>   and whoever curses you I will curse;
> and all peoples on earth
>   will be blessed through you. (Genesis 12:1–3 NIV)

Abram left home with his wife and nephew. After passing through the land God promised to give him, there was a severe famine, so Abram led his crew down to Egypt where there was food (Exodus 12:4–10).

> As he was about to enter Egypt, he said to his wife Sarai, "I know what a beautiful woman you are. When the Egyptians see you, they will say, 'This is his wife.' Then they will kill me but will let you live. Say you are my sister, so that I will be treated well for your sake and my life will be spared because of you." (Genesis 12:11–13 NIV)

Pharaoh indeed liked the look of Sarai (later called Sarah) and took her, but God struck Pharaoh's house with a plague until she was returned to Abram. Abram and family left intact and under escort with many gifts from Pharaoh (Genesis 12:14–20).

When Abraham journeyed to Gerar in the Negev years later, Abraham again claimed Sarah was his sister. King Abimelech took her, and history repeated itself (Genesis 20).

Discussion Questions

1. James 2:22–23 (NIV) says, "You see that his faith and his actions were working together, and his faith was made complete by what he did. And the scripture was fulfilled that says, 'Abraham believed God, and it was credited to him as righteousness,' and he was called God's friend."

   Looking at his whole life's picture, Abraham did fulfill this. But looking at these points in Abraham's story, does he seem a likely candidate to

   ○ Be an example of belief in God
   ○ Demonstrate being a blessing to others

2. Why or why not?

Verses

When Moses was a young man, he saw an Egyptian hitting a Hebrew. Moses was raised by the Pharaoh's daughter and educated in the Egyptian palace, but he knew that was really a Hebrew. Seeing this injustice, Moses made sure no one was looking and killed the Egyptian, burying him in the sand. The next day when he tried to break up a fight between two Hebrews, the offender said, *"Who made you ruler and judge over us? Are you thinking of killing me as you killed the Egyptian?"* (Exodus 2:14 NIV). Moses panicked, thinking that his murder had become public knowledge. The Pharaoh found out, tried to kill him, and Moses fled to Midian in the desert (Exodus 2:11–15; see also verses 5–10).

Years later, that pharaoh died. Moses was working as a humble shepherd when God appeared through a burning bush and rocked his world.

> So now, go. I am sending you to Pharaoh to bring my people the Israelites out of Egypt."

> But Moses said to God, "Who am I that I should go to Pharaoh and bring the Israelites out of Egypt?"

> And God said, "I will be with you. And this will be the sign to you that it is I who have sent you: When you have brought the people out of Egypt, you will worship God on this mountain." (Exodus 3:10–12 NIV)

Moses had numerous objections. God patiently answered before sending him on his way back to Egypt. God gave him sign after sign to show Pharaoh and the people God meant business and Moses truly spoke for Him. After all that, Moses still had one final hesitation.

> Moses raised another objection to God: "Master, please, I don't talk well. I've never been good with words, neither before nor after you spoke to me. I stutter and stammer."

> God said, "And who do you think made the human mouth? And who makes some mute, some deaf, some sighted, some blind? Isn't it I, God? So, get going. I'll be right there with you—with your mouth! I'll be right there to teach you what to say."

> He said, "Oh, Master, please! Send somebody else!"

> God got angry with Moses: "Don't you have a brother, Aaron the Levite? He's good with words, I know he is. He speaks very well. In fact, at this very moment he's on

his way to meet you. When he sees you he's going to be glad. You'll speak to him and tell him what to say. I'll be right there with you as you speak and with him as he speaks, teaching you step by step. He will speak to the people for you. He'll act as your mouth, but you'll decide what comes out of it. Now take this staff in your hand; you'll use it to do the signs." (Exodus 4:10–17 MSG)

Discussion Questions

1. At this point in Moses' story, does he seem a likely candidate to
   a. Convince a stubborn Pharaoh to let God's people go?
   b. Lead the unruly nation of Israel for forty years in the wilderness?
   c. Become God's mouthpiece to the people,
      i. giving them God's law,
      ii. instructions for the tabernacle, priesthood, and worship,
      iii. and writing the first five books of the Old Testament?

2. Why or why not?

Verses

Esther was a beautiful, obedient girl being raised by her uncle Mordecai. She did not change when the edict came that all beautiful girls would be taken to the palace to join the king's haram and possibly be chosen as the king's new queen. Even then, Esther obeyed Mordecai.

> Esther had not revealed her nationality and family background, because Mordecai had forbidden her to do so. (Esther 2:10 NIV)

Esther "found favor" with the eunuch in charge of the young ladies. He gave her special treatment, even advising her what to take with her the one night she had with the king (Esther 2:1–16). Even with all this favor, Esther remained humbly obedient.

> And this is how she would go to the king: Anything she wanted was given her to take with her from the harem to the king's palace … When the turn came for Esther (the young woman Mordecai had adopted, the daughter of his uncle Abihail) to go to the king, she asked for nothing other than what Hegai, the king's eunuch who was in charge of the harem, suggested. And Esther won the favor of everyone who saw her. (Esther 2:13, 15 NIV)

The king chose Esther above all the other virgins and made her queen, throwing a banquet in her honor, proclaiming a holiday, and giving lots of gifts. Still Esther did not forget the humble girl she was.

But Esther had kept secret her family background and nationality just as Mordecai had told her to do, for she continued to follow Mordecai's instructions as she had done when he was bringing her up. (Esther 2:20 NIV)

Discussion Questions

1. At this point in Esther's story, does she seem a likely candidate to
    a. Risk death to enter the king's presence uninvited twice?
    b. Tell the king, who banished his last queen in a temper, that his right-hand man was her enemy?
    c. Save her entire race from annihilation?

2. Why or why not?
3. God used all the people we've studied today and this week in Bible study. What are some ways God could use you?

Week 4: Digging Deeper

Study Focus

Jesus chose twelve men to follow Him, learn from Him, and to be key leaders in spreading His message and church after He ascended into heaven. Today we will study the following question.

*   What kind of men made up Jesus' core group of twelve disciples?

Verses

Now the names of the twelve apostles are these: The first, Simon, who is called Peter, and Andrew his brother; and James the son of Zebedee, and John his brother; Philip and Bartholomew; Thomas and Matthew the tax collector; James the son of Alphaeus, and Thaddaeus; Simon the Zealot, and Judas Iscariot, the one who betrayed Him. (Matthew 10:2–4 NASB)

Bartholomew was also known as Nathanael (John 1:45 ff.). Matthew was also called Levi (Luke 5:27–31). Thaddaeus was also known as "Judas, son of James" (Luke 6:16) and Lebbaeus (Matthew 10:3). Simon the Zealot was also known as "Simon the Canaanite" (Mark 3:18).

Judas Iscariot killed himself after betraying the Lord (Matthew 27:1–10) and was replaced by Matthias after Jesus' ascension in Acts 1:20–26.

Discussion Question

- If someone asked you to describe Jesus' disciples the three years they followed Him before Christ's death, what would you say?

Verses

The disciples came from a variety of backgrounds. Listen for the professions and social standing of the following disciples.

> As He was going along by the Sea of Galilee, He saw Simon [Peter] and Andrew, the brother of Simon, casting a net in the sea; for they were fishermen. And Jesus said to them, "Follow Me, and I will make you become fishers of men." Immediately they left their nets and followed Him. Going on a little farther, He saw James the son of Zebedee, and John his brother, who were also in the boat mending the nets. Immediately He called them; and they left their father Zebedee in the boat with the hired servants, and went away to follow Him. (Mark 1:16–20 NASB)

> After that He went out and noticed a tax collector named Levi sitting in the tax booth, and He said to him, "Follow Me." And he left everything behind, and got up and began to follow Him.

> And Levi gave a big reception for Him in his house; and there was a great crowd of tax collectors and other people who were reclining at the table with them. The Pharisees and their scribes began grumbling at His disciples, saying, "Why do you eat and drink with the tax collectors and sinners?" (Luke 5:27–30 NASB)

Simon the Canaanite was known as "the Zealot." Zealots were a highly religious group but distinct from the Pharisees or Sadducees. As Roman rule threatened traditional Jewish life more and more, Zealots were willing to fight in their advocacy of practicing the Jewish faith as prescribed in the Old Testament Law.

Discussion Questions

1. Would you categorize these men as extraordinary or ordinary before Jesus called them to follow Him? Why?

2. If the men Jesus chose to be His disciples were standing in a crowd, do you think you would have picked them out as Jesus did? Why or why not?

Verses

Simon the Zealot was not the only religious one of the bunch. Some of Jesus' disciples were first disciples of John the Baptist.

> Again the next day John was standing with two of his disciples, and he looked at Jesus as He walked, and said, "Behold, the Lamb of God!" The two disciples heard him speak, and they followed Jesus. And Jesus turned and saw them following, and said to them, "What do you seek?" They said to Him, "Rabbi (which translated means Teacher), where are You staying?" He said to them, "Come, and you will see." So they came and saw where He was staying; and they stayed with Him that day, for it was about the tenth hour. One of the two who heard John speak and followed Him, was Andrew, Simon Peter's brother. He found first his own brother Simon and said to him, "We have found the Messiah" (which translated means Christ). He brought him to Jesus. Jesus looked at him and said, "You are Simon the son of John; you shall be called Cephas" (which is translated Peter).
>
> The next day He purposed to go into Galilee, and He found Philip. And Jesus said to him, "Follow Me." Now Philip was from Bethsaida, of the city of Andrew and Peter. Philip found Nathanael and said to him, "We have found Him of whom Moses in the Law and also the Prophets wrote—Jesus of Nazareth, the son of Joseph" … Nathanael answered Him, "Rabbi, You are the Son of God; You are the King of Israel." (John 1:35–45, 49 NASB)

Discussion Question

• What is something you think Jesus' disciples may have had in common?

Verses

The disciples did not have any formal religious education, but after three years with Jesus, these common men were notably changed. Their boldness and assurance in what they taught caught the attention of even the Jewish council of leaders.

> Now as they observed the confidence of Peter and John and understood that they were uneducated and untrained men, they were amazed, and began to recognize them as having been with Jesus. (Acts 4:13 NASB)

Discussion Questions

1. What was it that changed these common men to extraordinary witnesses for Christ?
2. How can God take ordinary people like us and use us powerfully for Christ?
3. Do you think God could use you to be a hero or example to someone and not even be aware of it?
4. How do the things you learned today and this week in Bible study change the way you view yourself and your potential?
5. What will change in the way you live each day as a result of this perspective?

Week 4: On the Road Family Challenge Debrief (optional[5])

On the Road Family Challenge: Gather the family and read the following verses (use the table of contents or *www.biblegateway.com* if needed): Hebrews 11:1–2, 4–7, 17–26, 40. Then ask everyone this question: If you were anyone in the Bible, who would you be and why?

Encourage those who missed this week's On the Road Family Challenge to take advantage of each week's family learning experiences.

Discussion Questions

1. How did your On the Road Family Challenge go this week?
2. What Bible character would you be and why?
3. What other Bible characters came up in your family discussion?
4. Did you notice any common character traits in the people your family mentioned?
5. What are some unique traits in your family members that God could use for His glory?
6. What surprised you the most in this hunt?
7. What did you learn through this hunt?
8. Speaking to those who believe in Christ, 1 Peter 2:9 (NIV) says, "But you are a chosen people, a royal priesthood, a holy nation, a people belonging to God, that you may declare the praises of him who called you out of darkness." What is one thing God may be asking you to do this week?
9. (If you have time) What are some ways we can teach our children to see the potential in themselves and others around them?

Week 5: Who Is Jesus?

Either this man was, and is, the Son of God:
or else a madman or something worse.
You can shut Him up for a fool, you can spit at Him and kill Him as a demon;
or you can fall at His feet and call Him Lord and God.
But let us not come with any patronizing nonsense
about His being a great human teacher."

C. S. Lewis[19]

Week 5: Prayer Focus

We did not follow cleverly invented stories when we told you about the power and coming of our Lord Jesus Christ, but we were eyewitnesses of his majesty. (2 Peter 1:16 NIV)

God is real, and so is Jesus Christ. We have eyewitness accounts of Jesus' life, ministry, and death here on earth as well as reports of those who have had life-changing encounters with Him today. Praise God! Are there any special praises or prayer requests this week?

End your prayer time thanking God for showing Himself to you.

Week 5: Review and Application

Discussion Question

- Why do you think humankind keeps trying to put God in a box we can measure and understand?

Verses

"For my thoughts are not your thoughts,
neither are your ways my ways,"

declares the LORD.

"As the heavens are higher than the earth,
  so are my ways higher than your ways
  and my thoughts than your thoughts." (Isaiah 55:8–9 NIV)

God is God, and we are not. He cannot be limited by what we know, can measure, or comprehend. However, God has always wanted us to know and understand Him. First of all, He revealed Himself to us in the Bible, which is also called His Revelation, Word, or Law.

The secret things belong to the LORD our God, but the things revealed belong to us and to our children forever, that we may follow all the words of this law. (Deuteronomy 29:29 NIV)

God has promised that if we seek to learn, know, and understand Him better, He will teach us (Psalm 25:4–5; Isaiah 55:6; James 1:5). He *wants* to us to know Him even as He knows us. He wants to have a relationship with us. He wants us to seek Him.

The fool says in his heart,
  "There is no God."
They are corrupt, and their ways are vile;
  There is no one who goes good.
God looks down from heaven
  On the sons of men
To see if there are any who understand
  Any who seek God. (Psalm 53:1–2 NIV)

Discussion Question

- Can we ever see or touch God? Why or why not?

Verses

A few people in the Bible asked to see God, to put material substance behind their belief. Some had the opportunity without asking.

Moses asked to see God's glory. He had been hearing God's voice for some time and wanted to put a face or image to what he was learning. It was understandable. Moses was raised in Egypt, where there were statues of the various gods of their religion everywhere. Moses must have just assumed that Yahweh, the great I AM who had proved He was greater than all the gods of Egypt, had a form, too, and was curious what animal/human combination or other form He might take.[20] Maybe it would be something with flames like the burning bush that first appeared to him. The answer he got must have shocked him.

> And the LORD [Yahweh] said, "I will cause all my goodness to pass in front of you, and I will proclaim my name, the LORD [Yahweh], in your presence. I will have mercy on whom I will have mercy, and I will have compassion on whom I will have compassion. But," he said, "you cannot see my face, for no one may see me and live." (Exodus 33:19–20 NIV)

God covered Moses with His hand in a cleft in the rock until His glory passed by. He uncovered Moses to allow him to see the Lord's back so he would not die.

Isaiah saw the Lord on His throne, "high and exalted." He describes the train of the Lord's throne filling the temple, the heavenly creatures praising God in the throne room (whose voices shook the doorposts), the smoke that filled the room, and the Lord's voice. Isaiah also describes his immediate, personal awareness of his sin and unworthiness to be there. This was taken care of by an act atoning (making payment) for his sins (Isaiah 6:1–8). Like Moses, Isaiah never saw the Lord's face.

Discussion Question

- How do you think you would react if you suddenly found yourself in God's presence?

Verses

All this changed when Jesus was born. In Jesus, God did something amazing. Jesus was God in the flesh! He became a God we could see, touch, relate to, and better understand. Because of Jesus, we can come face to face with God Himself.

> Philip said, "Lord, show us the Father and that will be enough for us."

> Jesus answered: "Don't you know me, Philip, even after I have been among you such a long time? Anyone who has seen me has seen the Father. How can you say, 'Show us the Father'?" (John 14:8–9 NIV)

Not only is Jesus God in the flesh, but His death also paid the price for our sins so we can come confidently into the throne room of God Almighty.

> For this reason Christ is the mediator of a new covenant, that those who are called may receive the promised eternal inheritance—now that he has died as a ransom to set them free from the sins committed under the first covenant. (Hebrews 9:15 NIV)

Therefore, brothers and sisters, since we have confidence to enter the Most Holy Place by the blood of Jesus … let us draw near to God with a sincere heart and with the full assurance that faith brings, having our hearts sprinkled to cleanse us from a guilty conscience and having our bodies washed with pure water. Let us hold unswervingly to the hope we profess, for he who promised is faithful. (Hebrews 10:19, 22–23 NIV)

Think of yourselves the way Christ Jesus thought of himself. He had equal status with God but didn't think so much of himself that he had to cling to the advantages of that status no matter what. Not at all. When the time came, he set aside the privileges of deity and took on the status of a slave, became *human*! Having become human, he stayed human. It was an incredibly humbling process. He didn't claim special privileges. Instead, he lived a selfless, obedient life and then died a selfless, obedient death—and the worst kind of death at that—a crucifixion.

Because of that obedience, God lifted him high and honored him far beyond anyone or anything, ever, so that all created beings in heaven and on earth—even those long ago dead and buried—will bow in worship before this Jesus Christ, and call out in praise that he is the Master of all, to the glorious honor of God the Father (Philippians 2:6–11 MSG; emphasis in original).

Discussion Questions

1. Why is Jesus so important?
2. How will what you have learned today and this week in Bible study change the way you approach God every day?

Week 5: Digging Deeper

Study Focus

This week in Bible study we talked a lot about how Jesus is fully God, but He is also fully man. Today we will study the following question:

- How do we know that Jesus was human just like us?

Discussion Question

- If you are willing, share something you remember from the birth of one of your children.

Verses

Although Jesus was miraculously conceived by God in a virgin's womb (Matthew 1:8, 24–25; Luke 1:26–38), Mary gave birth to baby Jesus in the same way as so many mothers before her. "While they were there, the days were completed for her to give birth. And she gave birth to her firstborn son; and she wrapped Him in cloths, and laid Him in a manger, because there was no room for them in the inn" (Luke 2:6–7 NASB).

Jesus was circumcised[21] at eight days old, just like any other Jewish boy (Luke 2:21–24, 39), and had to grow and learn through childhood and the teenage years like the rest of us. "The Child continued to grow and become strong, increasing in wisdom; and the grace of God was upon Him" (Luke 2:40 NASB; see also verse 52). Luke 2:41–51 tells of a time when twelve-year-old Jesus sat in the temple courts in Jerusalem, listening and asking the teachers questions to learn all that He could.

Jesus' friends and neighbors from his youth had trouble believing in His words and works, for they only saw Him as a man, the carpenter's son. They were also hung up on seeing Him in His human place among His mother, brothers, and sisters still living in Nazareth (Matthew 13:53–58). "And they took offense at Him" (Matthew 13:57 NASB).

Jesus got hungry (Matthew 4:2), thirsty (John 19:28), and tired, just like us. "So Jesus, being wearied from His journey, was sitting thus by the well" (John 4:6 NASB). The day He died, Jesus was beaten so badly He could not carry His cross to the place of His execution. Someone else had to carry it for Him (Matthew 26:67–68; 27:26–32).

Following His resurrection, Jesus allowed Thomas to see for himself that He still was still a man with a physical body. "See My hands and My feet, that it is I Myself; touch Me and see, for a spirit does not have flesh and bones as you see that I have" (Luke 24:39 NASB).

Discussion Question

• What are some emotions all human beings experience?

Verses

Jesus experienced the full range of human emotions.

> Then he said to them, "My soul is overwhelmed with sorrow to the point of death. Stay here and keep watch with me." (Matthew 26:38 NIV).

After he had said this, Jesus was troubled in spirit and testified, "Very truly I tell you, one of you is going to betray me." (John 13:21 NIV; see also John 12:27)

When Jesus heard this, he was amazed and said to those following him, "Truly I tell you, I have not found anyone in Israel with such great faith." (Matthew 8:10 NIV)

During the days of Jesus' life on earth, he offered up prayers and petitions with fervent cries and tears to the one who could save him from death, and he was heard because of his reverent submission. (Hebrews 5:7 NIV)

When Lazarus died, his sisters sent for their good friend Jesus. He arrived to encounter their grief in full swing and was deeply moved. "When Jesus therefore saw her weeping, and the Jews who came with her also weeping, He was deeply moved in spirit and was troubled, and said, 'Where have you laid him?' They said to Him, 'Lord, come and see.' Jesus wept. So the Jews were saying, 'See how He loved him!'" (John 11:33–36 NASB).

Jesus also got angry. Anger itself is not a sin, but often the things we do while we're angry are sins (Ephesians 4:25–27). At the beginning and end of Jesus' public ministry, He entered the temple of Jerusalem and drove the money changers and sellers out of the place, overturning their tables (John 2:12–25; Mark 11:15–19).[22] "To those who sold doves he said, 'Get these out of here! Stop turning my Father's house into a market!' His disciples remembered that it is written: 'Zeal for your house will consume me'" (John 2:16–17 NIV).

Discussion Question

- When you've gotten angry or emotional in the past, have you been tempted to do something you'd regret (sin)? Did you actually do it, or did you catch yourself and not?

Verses

Just before His public ministry began, Jesus went into the wilderness to fast and pray. When He was fully weakened by His fast, Satan himself came to tempt Jesus. He began by reaching out to Jesus' physical needs.

And after He had fasted forty days and forty nights, He then became hungry. And the tempter came and said to Him, "If You are the Son of God, command that these stones become bread." But He answered and said, "It is written, 'Man shall not live on bread alone, but on every word that proceeds out of the mouth of God.'" (Matthew 4:2–4 NASB)

In all the ways Satan tempted Jesus, He never sinned, not even as a child or later in His ministry.

Speaking of Jesus, Hebrews 4:15 (NASB) says, "For we do not have a high priest who cannot sympathize with our weaknesses, but One who has been tempted in all things as we are, yet without sin."

Discussion Question

- Why do you think it's so important that Jesus was fully human yet without sin?

Verses

Therefore, since the children share in flesh and blood, He Himself likewise also partook of the same, that through death He might render powerless him who had the power of death, that is, the devil, and might free those who through fear of death were subject to slavery all their lives. (Hebrews 2:14–15 NASB)

Jesus became fully human and faced every temptation we face, but without sin. Because of that, He could pay the penalty for sin—death (Romans 6:23). We'll be talking about that more this week in the daily Bible study and next week in small group.

Invite those who have questions today to talk to you after group. A guide to talking to individuals about asking Jesus to be your Lord and Savior may be found on page 80.]

Discussion Question

- How does seeing Jesus as fully human, but without sin, change the way you approach Him?

Week 5: On the Road Family Challenge Debrief (optional[5])

On the Road Family Challenge: This is the week to find out where your family stands. Ask your kids, "What do you know about Jesus?" If you're comfortable, follow it up with a conversation. If not, just thank them for sharing and remember their answer(s) to follow up later.

Encourage those who missed this week's On the Road Family Challenge to take advantage of each week's family learning experiences.

Discussion Questions

1. How did your On the Road Family Challenge go this week?
2. What did you expect your family to know about Jesus going into your On the Road Family Challenge this week?
3. Did your family meet, exceed, or fall short of your expectations?
4. What surprised you the most in this hunt?
5. What did you learn through this hunt?
6. Where may your family hear about Jesus (true or false information about Him)?
7. What kinds of false information about Jesus may your family hear from different influences around you?
8. Have you or someone you know been challenged on what you believe? What happened?
9. What are some ways you can prepare your family to recognize false information when they encounter it?
10. "Preach the word; be prepared in season and out of season; correct, rebuke and encourage—with great patience and careful instruction. For the time will come when people will not put up with sound doctrine. Instead, to suit their own desires, they will gather around them a great number of teachers to say what their itching ears want to hear. They will turn their ears away from the truth and turn aside to myths" (2 Timothy 4:2–4, NIV). Do you feel prepared to counter false information you hear about Jesus Christ? If not, how might you become better prepared?
11. (If you have time) What are some ways we can teach our children to combat the untruths they encounter about Jesus Christ?

Week 6: How Can You Be Changed?

In other words, the Christian life is one of faith,
where we find ourselves routinely overdriving our headlights
but knowing it's okay because God is in control
and has a purpose behind it.

Bill Hybels and Mark Mittelberg[23]

Week 6: Prayer Focus

Who foretold this long ago,
    who declared it from the distant past?
Was it not I, the LORD?
    And there is no God apart from me,
a righteous God and a Savior;
    there is none but me.
Turn to me and be saved,
    all you ends of the earth;
    for I am God, and there is no other. (Isaiah 45:21–22 NIV)

The almighty God loves you. He had a plan to pay for your sin once and for all from the very beginning of time.

Are there any special praises or prayer requests this week?

End your prayer time asking God to touch the hearts of those who need to know Him.

Week 6: Review and Application

Discussion Question

- What are some things you've heard taught to you or in the world about what happens after we die?

Facts: Many religions are based on doing enough of the right things to either counter the wrong things we do or earn enough credit to get to a better place.

Wicca (witchcraft) is a growing practice in North America today, especially among teenagers.[24] Wiccans worship a mother goddess and her consort, a male, horned deity. They believe in one or more of three things.

1) Animism: The belief that everything—people, animals, plants, and inanimate objects (like rocks, wind, and rain)—has a soul and spirit.
2) Pantheism: The belief that either everything is god (pantheism) or that God is in everything (panentheism).
3) Polytheism: There is more than one god. This often leads to reasoning like, "There is no one way or right religion for all," and, "There is no one truth."[25]

Other philosophies and religions come to similar conclusions that there is no one standard of truth or that all roads lead to the same end. Still others swing the other way and claim this world is all there is, and there is no God.

Discussion Question

- What do you think happens when we die? (There is no wrong answer.)

What if you were wrong? Would you really want to wait until you were dead, and it was too late to be confronted with your error? (Response not required.)

Verses:

In response to earning a place in heaven, the Bible says,

> For it is by grace you have been saved, through faith—and this is not from yourselves, it is the gift of God—not by works, so that no one can boast. (Ephesians 2:8–9 NIV)

And if by grace, then it cannot be based on works; if it were, grace would no longer be grace. (Romans 11:6 NIV)

In response to pantheism (the belief that everything is god) and panentheism (the belief that God is in everything), the Bible describes God creating everything that is not God.

> In the beginning God created the heavens and the earth. (Genesis 1:1 NIV)

And God said, "Let the land produce living creatures according to their kinds … [rather than according to God's "kind"]." (Genesis 1:24 NIV)

In response to animism (the belief that everything has a soul and spirit), the Bible shows a distinction between humanity and the rest of creation.

Genesis 1 follows a pattern: God spoke, and it was so. That is how light, sky, land, plants, sun, moon, stars, and every living thing was created—everything except man and woman. "Then the LORD God formed a man from the dust of the ground and breathed into his nostrils the breath of life, and the man became a living being" (Genesis 2:7 NIV). Woman He formed from the rib of the man (Genesis 2:21–23).

Only humankind is created with a soul to live in a right relationship with God Almighty: "And now, Israel, what does the LORD your God ask of you but to fear the LORD your God, to walk in obedience to him, to love him, to serve the LORD your God with all your heart and with all your soul, and to observe the LORD's commands and decrees that I am giving you today for your own good?" (Deuteronomy 10:12–13, NIV).

In response to polytheism (the belief that there is more than one god), the Bible says,

> Hear, O Israel! The LORD is our God, the LORD is one! (Deuteronomy 6:4 NASB)

> This is what the LORD says—
>   Israel's King and Redeemer, the LORD Almighty:
> I am the first and I am the last;
>   apart from me there is no God. (Isaiah 44:6 NIV; see also Isaiah 43:10)

In response to claims that there is no God and this world is all there is, God's Word says,

> By myself I have sworn,
>   my mouth has uttered in all integrity
>   a word that will not be revoked:
>   Before me every knee will bow;
>   by me every tongue will swear.
>   They will say of me, "In the LORD alone
>   are deliverance and strength."
> All who have raged against him
>   will come to him and be put to shame." (Isaiah 45:23–24 NIV)

Jesus obeyed the Father and humbled Himself, becoming human and dying on the cross for us (Philippians 2:5–8).

> Therefore God exalted him to the highest place
>   and gave him the name that is above every name,
> that at the name of Jesus every knee should bow,
>   in heaven and on earth and under the earth,
> and every tongue acknowledge that Jesus Christ is Lord,
>   to the glory of God the Father. (Philippians 2:9–11 NIV)

In response to the idea that there is no one standard of truth or that all roads lead to the same end, the Bible says,

> Jesus said, "I am the Road, also the Truth, also the Life. No one gets to the Father apart from me. If you really knew me, you would know my Father as well. From now on, you do know him. You've even seen him!" (John 14:6–7 MSG)

Discussion Questions

1. Have you ever made a decision to follow Jesus as your Lord and Savior? If not, what is stopping you from making that decision today? (Encourage those in your group not comfortable making a public decision to talk to you privately to learn more about making Jesus their Lord and Savior. See page 80 for help in talking to someone about Christ.)
2. How has what you've learned today or this week in Bible study challenged or affirmed what you knew about Jesus or the Bible?

Week 6: Digging Deeper

Study Focus

Jesus is often called the "Lamb of God." This term has deep roots in the Old Testament. Today we will study the following question:

- How does Jesus fulfill the Passover and Old Testament sacrificial system?

Verses

> In fact, the law requires that nearly everything be cleansed with blood, and without the shedding of blood there is no forgiveness [of sin]. (Hebrews 9:22 NIV)

The first animal sacrifice was when God killed the first living creatures to make skin garments for Adam and Eve following the first sin (Genesis 3:21). Animal sacrifices continue as an act of worship through Genesis (i.e., 8:20–21), until the practice is formalized in Exodus, when Moses gives God's law to the people of Israel. It begins with the Passover Lamb.

Discussion Question

- What do you know about the situation in Egypt just before the Israelites were set free from slavery?

Verses

Hebrews had been cruelly enslaved in Egypt for four hundred years. God had heard their cries for release and was about to free them from Egyptian bondage. Moses came at God's command to tell Pharaoh, "Let My people go." Pharaoh said no and made the Hebrews' workload harder, so Moses announced a plague from God. After nine plagues, God was about to demonstrate His power one final time (Genesis 15:13; Exodus 2:23–25; 5–11:1). This time it included things He wanted those who trusted in Him to do as well.

God was going to send an angel of death over the land to kill all of the firstborn, from that of Pharaoh to that of the lowest servant. Even the first born of the cattle would be killed (Exodus 11:4–5). In order to show the power of God and save those who trusted in the God of the Hebrews, God provided instructions for them to follow.

Each family was to take a male lamb without any imperfections, keep it and watch it for two weeks. Then they were to kill it at twilight on the same day. Some of the lamb's blood was to be put on the lintel and doorframe of the house where they would spend the night eating a special meal, featuring the lamb, roasted whole with no broken bones (Exodus 12:3–12, 46).

> The blood will be a sign for you on the houses where you are, and when I see the blood, I will pass over you. No destructive plague will touch you when I strike Egypt. (Exodus 12:13 NIV)

Discussion Question

- What other kinds of offerings were given in the Old Testament?

Verses

God told Moses in Exodus 20:24 (NASB), "You shall make an altar of earth for Me, and you shall sacrifice on it your burnt offerings and your peace offerings, your sheep and your oxen; in every place where I cause My name to be remembered, I will come to you and bless you."

Leviticus 4–5 describes the burnt offerings required from individuals as a penalty for their sins. They are all lambs, bulls, or rams (unless one cannot afford a lamb).

Leviticus 3 describes the law of peace offerings. These offerings are sometimes called "soothing aromas" before the Lord. "But if his offering for a sacrifice of peace offerings to the LORD is from the flock, he shall offer it, male or female, without defect. If he is going to offer a lamb for his offering, then he shall offer it before the LORD, and he shall lay his hand on the head of his offering and slay it before the tent of meeting, and Aaron's sons shall sprinkle its blood around on the altar" (Leviticus 3:6–8, NASB).

Discussion Question

- In what ways is Jesus the Passover lamb, the lamb of sacrifice?

Verses

Jesus came to earth to become like us, one of the flock of sheep, so He could be used for sacrifice.

> We all, like sheep, have gone astray,
>   each of us has turned to our own way;
> and the LORD has laid on him
>   the iniquity of us all.
> He was oppressed and afflicted,
>   yet he did not open his mouth;
> he was led like a lamb to the slaughter,
>   and as a sheep before its shearers is silent,
>   so he did not open his mouth. (Isaiah 53:6–7 NIV)

Like the Passover lamb, Jesus lived among the people for a short time before He died, so they could see He was without blemish or sin (John 8:46; 2 Corinthians 5:21). Not one of His bones was broken when He died at Passover (John 19:30–36).

First Corinthians 5:7–8 calls Jesus the "Passover Lamb" and reminds us to clean out sin in our lives just as in the celebration of the Passover, people rid their homes of yeast. This is because Jesus Christ is the sacrificial Lamb, whose blood makes it possible for us to escape death and be freed from the bondage of sin.

> For you know that it was not with perishable things such as silver or gold that you were redeemed from the empty way of life handed down to you from your ancestors, but with the precious blood of Christ, a lamb without blemish or defect. (1 Peter 1:18–19 NIV)

John the Baptist calls Jesus the "Lamb of God" in his preaching by the Jordan River and when he finally met the Lord face to face (John 1:29 ff. NIV). This title reappears in Revelation, when Jesus is worshipped as the Lamb in heaven. Listen to the worship that surrounds the Lamb and the reasons He is praised:

> So I looked, and there, surrounded by Throne, Animals, and Elders, was a Lamb, slaughtered but standing tall. Seven horns he had, and seven eyes, the Seven Spirits of God sent into all the earth. He came to the One Seated on the Throne and took the scroll from his right hand. The moment he took the scroll, the Four Animals and Twenty-four Elders fell down and worshiped the Lamb. Each had a harp and each had a bowl, a gold bowl filled with incense, the prayers of God's holy people. And they sang a new song:

> > Worthy! Take the scroll, open its seals.
> > Slain! Paying in blood, you bought men and women,
> > Bought them back from all over the earth,
> > Bought them back for God.
> > Then you made them a Kingdom, Priests for our God,
> > Priest-kings to rule over the earth.

> I looked again. I heard a company of Angels around the Throne, the Animals, and the Elders—ten thousand times ten thousand their number, thousand after thousand after thousand in full song:

> > The slain Lamb is worthy!
> > Take the power, the wealth, the wisdom, the strength!
> > Take the honor, the glory, the blessing!

> Then I heard every creature in Heaven and earth, in underworld and sea, join in, all voices in all places, singing:

> To the One on the Throne! To the Lamb!
> The blessing, the honor, the glory, the strength,
> For age after age after age.

The Four Animals called out, "Oh, Yes!" The Elders fell to their knees and worshiped. (Revelation 5:6–14 MSG)

Jesus paid for sin once and for all. His blood made it possible for God's punishment of death to pass over us. Because of what Jesus did, we no longer have to continue making offerings to pay for our sin. All we have to do is accept the gift of forgiveness He offers us: He has a stamp marked "Paid in Full," inked in His blood and ready to apply to the sin in your life.

Discussion Questions

1. Have you ever accepted Jesus' gift to pay for your sins, wash them in His blood, and take them away forever?
2. If not, is that something you would like to do today?

   (Be sure to make yourself available to talk to anyone interested in learning more about a relationship with Christ. A guide for leading someone to Christ is available on page 80.)

3. How would including worship of the Lamb into your life change how you live each day?

Week 6: On the Road Family Challenge Debrief (optional[5])

On the Road Family Challenge: Do you remember asking your kids what they knew about Jesus? This is your week to follow up on those conversations. Take the first few days to pray for these conversations. Then talk with your kids about who Jesus is and what He did for us.

Encourage those who missed this week's On the Road Family Challenge to take advantage of each week's family learning experiences.

Discussion Questions

1. How did your On the Road Family Challenge go this week?
2. Did you feel prepared to talk to your children about Christ?

3. What might help you feel better prepared to talk to your children about Christ in the future?

4. What advice would you give to someone else thinking about talking to their children about Jesus?

5. "How, then, can they call on the one they have not believed in? And how can they believe in the one of whom they have not heard? And how can they hear without someone preaching to them? And how can anyone preach unless they are sent? As it is written: 'How beautiful are the feet of those who bring good news!'" (Romans 10:14–15 NIV).

   Did you get a chance to lead any of your children to Christ? If so, tell us about it.

6. Have you ever had a time when you asked Jesus to be your Lord and Savior? If so, tell us about it.

7. What next step may God be asking you to take?

8. (If you have time) What are some ways we can make conversations about Jesus with our children a regular part of our daily routines?

Week 7: How Can a Family Follow God?

Sometimes I just have to be reminded that what I give to my children
or what I do for my children is not as important as what I leave in them.
Isn't it interesting how 'stuff' can distract us from what is really valuable
and how quickly we can get confused about what it means to be rich?

Reggie Joiner[26]

Week 7: Prayer Focus

Attention, Israel! God, our God! God the one and only! Love God, your God, with your whole heart: love him with all that's in you, love him with all you've got! Write these commandments that I've given you today on your hearts. Get them inside of you and then get them inside your children. Talk about them wherever you are, sitting at home or walking in the street; talk about them from the time you get up in the morning to when you fall into bed at night. Tie them on your hands and foreheads as a reminder; inscribe them on the doorposts of your homes and on your city gates. (Deuteronomy 6:4–9 MSG)

God deserves and wants first place in our hearts and lives. He encourages us to do whatever it takes to remind ourselves and our families of that as we go through each day.

Are there any special praises or prayer requests this week?

End your prayer time praising God and dedicating your life and your family to Him.

Week 7: Review and Application

Discussion Question

1. How do you keep track of the days of the week, your family's schedule and appointments?
2. How do you remember what errands to run, what to buy at the store, and things like that?

3. How do you approach planning for birthday parties or holidays?
4. What is the system in your family to know whether the dishes are clean or dirty?

Lists and reminders help us remember things we don't want to forget in the busyness of life. They also help us remember to communicate important information to others.

Verses

Jacob first personally encountered the Lord in a dream. In that dream, God renewed the promise He had made to Abraham and Isaac, Jacob's father and grandfather.

> Then Jacob awoke from his sleep and said, "Surely the LORD is in this place, and I did not know it." He was afraid and said, "How awesome is this place! This is none other than the house of God, and this is the gate of heaven." So Jacob rose early in the morning, and took the stone that he had put under his head and set it up as a pillar and poured oil on its top. He called the name of that place Bethel [house of God]; however, previously the name of the city had been Luz. Then Jacob made a vow, saying, "If God will be with me and will keep me on this journey that I take, and will give me food to eat and garments to wear, and I return to my father's house in safety, then the LORD will be my God. This stone, which I have set up as a pillar, will be God's house, and of all that You give me I will surely give a tenth to You." (Genesis 28:16–22 NASB)

When the nation of Israel entered the Promised Land, God dried up the Jordan River, so they could cross over on dry land. This was a powerful act of God He didn't want them to ever forget (Joshua 3:1–4:3).

> So Joshua called the twelve men whom he had appointed from the sons of Israel, one man from each tribe; and Joshua said to them, "Cross again to the ark of the LORD your God into the middle of the Jordan, and each of you take up a stone on his shoulder, according to the number of the tribes of the sons of Israel. Let this be a sign among you, so that when your children ask later, saying, 'What do these stones mean to you?' then you shall say to them, 'Because the waters of the Jordan were cut off before the ark of the covenant of the LORD; when it crossed the Jordan, the waters of the Jordan were cut off.' So these stones shall become a memorial to the sons of Israel forever." (Joshua 4:4–7 NASB)

Discussion Question

1. What are some ways God has worked in the lives of your family members?
2. What are some reminders you can create to remember these things, maybe in a way that others might ask about them?

Verses

Moses said to the people, "Remember this day in which you went out from Egypt, from the house of slavery; for by a powerful hand the LORD brought you out from this place. And nothing leavened shall be eaten. On this day in the month of Abib, you are about to go forth. It shall be when the LORD brings you to the land of the Canaanite, the Hittite, the Amorite, the Hivite and the Jebusite, which He swore to your fathers to give you, a land flowing with milk and honey, that you shall observe this rite in this month. For seven days you shall eat unleavened bread, and on the seventh day there shall be a feast to the LORD. Unleavened bread shall be eaten throughout the seven days; and nothing leavened shall be seen among you, nor shall any leaven be seen among you in all your borders. You shall tell your son on that day, saying, 'It is because of what the LORD did for me when I came out of Egypt.' And it shall serve as a sign to you on your hand, and as a reminder on your forehead, that the law of the LORD may be in your mouth; for with a powerful hand the LORD brought you out of Egypt. Therefore, you shall keep this ordinance at its appointed time from year to year." (Exodus 13:3–10 NASB)

Discussion Question

- How can you incorporate reminders of God and His works into upcoming holidays?

Verses

Now when the LORD brings you to the land of the Canaanite, as He swore to you and to your fathers, and gives it to you, you shall devote to the LORD the first offspring of every womb, and the first offspring of every beast that you own; the males belong to the LORD. But every first offspring of a donkey you shall redeem with a lamb, but if you do not redeem it, then you shall break its neck; and every firstborn of man among your sons you shall redeem. And it shall be when your son asks you in time to come, saying, "What is this?" then you shall say to him, "With a powerful hand the LORD brought us out of Egypt, from the house of slavery. It came about, when Pharaoh was stubborn about letting us go, that the LORD killed every firstborn in the land of Egypt, both the firstborn of man and the firstborn of beast. Therefore, I sacrifice to the LORD the males, the first offspring of every womb, but every firstborn of my sons I redeem." So it shall serve as a sign on your hand and as phylacteries on your forehead, for with a powerful hand the LORD brought us out of Egypt. (Exodus 13:11–16 NASB)

Christ redeemed us when He died on the cross to pay for our sins (Colossians 1:15–23), but we still bring our tithes and offerings as reminders of the blessings God gives us (Malachi 3:8–15).

Discussion Question

1. What regular habits can you use to remind yourself and your family of who God is and how He works in your life?
2. What is one thing you can set up or start this week to help your family remember how God works powerfully in people's lives?

Week 7: Digging Deeper

Study Focus

Jesus prayed for His disciples: "My prayer is not that you take them out of the world but that you protect them from the evil one. They are not of the world, even as I am not of it. Sanctify them by the truth; your word is truth. As you sent me into the world, I have sent them into the world. For them I sanctify myself, that they too may be truly sanctified" (John 17:15–19 NIV). From this we get the saying, "In the world, but not of the world." Today we will study the following question:

- How can we be "in the world, but not of the world"?

Verses

If you belonged to the world, it would love you as its own. As it is, you do not belong to the world, but I have chosen you out of the world. That is why the world hates you. (John 15:19 NIV)

Do not love the world or anything in the world. If anyone loves the world, love for the Father is not in them. For everything in the world—the lust of the flesh, the lust of the eyes, and the pride of life—comes not from the Father but from the world. The world and its desires pass away, but whoever does the will of God lives forever. (1 John 2:15–17 NIV)

I have told you these things, so that in me you may have peace. In this world you will have trouble. But take heart! I have overcome the world. (John 16:33 NIV)

Consider it pure joy, my brothers and sisters, whenever you face trials of many kinds, because you know that the testing of your faith produces perseverance. Let perseverance finish its work so that you may be mature and complete, not lacking anything. If any of you lacks wisdom, you should ask God, who gives generously to all without finding fault, and it will be given to you. But when you ask, you must believe and not doubt, because the one who doubts is like a wave of the sea, blown and tossed by the wind. That person should not expect to receive anything from the Lord. Such a person is double-minded and unstable in all they do. (James 1:2–8 NIV)

When you ask, you do not receive, because you ask with wrong motives, that you may spend what you get on your pleasures. You adulterous people, don't you know that friendship with the world means enmity against God? Therefore, anyone who chooses to be a friend of the world becomes an enemy of God. Or do you think Scripture says without reason that he jealously longs for the spirit he has caused to dwell in us? But he gives us more grace. That is why Scripture says: "God opposes the proud but shows favor to the humble." (James 4:3–6 NIV)

See to it that no one takes you captive through hollow and deceptive philosophy, which depends on human tradition and the elemental spiritual forces of this world rather than on Christ. (Colossians 2:8 NIV)

Has not God made foolish the wisdom of the world? For since in the wisdom of God the world through its wisdom did not know him, God was pleased through the foolishness of what was preached to save those who believe. Jews demand signs and Greeks look for wisdom, but we preach Christ crucified: a stumbling block to Jews and foolishness to Gentiles, but to those whom God has called, both Jews and Greeks, Christ the power of God and the wisdom of God. For the foolishness of God is wiser than human wisdom, and the weakness of God is stronger than human strength. (1 Corinthians 1:20–25 NIV)

Therefore, I urge you, brothers and sisters, in view of God's mercy, to offer your bodies as a living sacrifice, holy and pleasing to God—this is your true and proper worship. Do not conform to the pattern of this world, but be transformed by the renewing of your mind. Then you will be able to test and approve what God's will is—his good, pleasing and perfect will. (Romans 12:1–2 NIV)

Discussion Questions

1. What are some dangers of being "in the world"?
2. How do some people respond to those possible dangers?
3. In the cautions about those dangers, did God ever say to leave the world?

Verses

He has shown you, O mortal, what is good.
    And what does the LORD require of you?
To act justly and to love mercy
    and to walk humbly with your God. (Micah 6:8 NIV)

On one occasion an expert in the law stood up to test Jesus. "Teacher," he asked, "what must I do to inherit eternal life?"

"What is written in the Law?" he replied. "How do you read it?"

He answered, "Love the Lord your God with all your heart and with all your soul and with all your strength and with all your mind"; and, "Love your neighbor as yourself."

"You have answered correctly," Jesus replied. "Do this and you will live."

But he wanted to justify himself, so he asked Jesus, "And who is my neighbor?"

In reply Jesus said: "A man was going down from Jerusalem to Jericho, when he was attacked by robbers. They stripped him of his clothes, beat him and went away, leaving him half dead. A priest happened to be going down the same road, and when he saw the man, he passed by on the other side. So too, a Levite, when he came to the place and saw him, passed by on the other side. But a Samaritan, as he traveled, came where the man was; and when he saw him, he took pity on him. He went to him and bandaged his wounds, pouring on oil and wine. Then he put the man on his own donkey, brought him to an inn and took care of him. The next day he took out two denarii and gave them to the innkeeper. 'Look after him,' he said, 'and when I return, I will reimburse you for any extra expense you may have.'

Which of these three do you think was a neighbor to the man who fell into the hands of robbers?"

The expert in the law replied, "The one who had mercy on him."

Jesus told him, "Go and do likewise." (Luke 10:25–37 NIV)

The King will reply, "Truly I tell you, whatever you did for one of the least of these brothers and sisters of mine, you did for me."

Then he will say to those on his left, "Depart from me, you who are cursed, into the eternal fire prepared for the devil and his angels. For I was hungry and you gave me nothing to eat, I was thirsty and you gave me nothing to drink, I was a stranger and you did not invite me in, I needed clothes and you did not clothe me, I was sick and in prison and you did not look after me."

They also will answer, "Lord, when did we see you hungry or thirsty or a stranger or needing clothes or sick or in prison, and did not help you?"

He will reply, "Truly I tell you, whatever you did not do for one of the least of these, you did not do for me."

Then they will go away to eternal punishment, but the righteous to eternal life. (Matthew 25:40–46 NIV)

Discussion Question

- What are some things God has called us to do "in the world"?

Verses

Religion that God our Father accepts as pure and faultless is this: to look after orphans and widows in their distress and to keep oneself from being polluted by the world. (James 1:27 NIV)

Jesus replied: "Love the Lord your God with all your heart and with all your soul and with all your mind. This is the first and greatest commandment. And the second is like it: Love your neighbor as yourself. All the Law and the Prophets hang on these two commandments." (Matthew 22:37–38 NIV)

Discussion Question

- Is there a different approach your family might need to take to being "in the world, but not of the world"?

Week 7: On the Road Family Challenge Debrief (optional[5])

On the Road Family Challenge: This world offers many distractions and opinions of how we should spend our time and where we should go to find the answers to our questions.

Decide as a family to put God first and to turn to the Bible for answers. Write the following verse on a paper or poster. (You can also look it up and do the whole verse.) *"But as for me and my household, we will serve the LORD"* (Joshua 24:15 NIV). Decorate it and have everyone sign it. Then hang it where all can see it.

Discuss what it would look like in each of your lives to keep God first. Set up a "secret code" to remind members of your family to keep God first (e.g., "How's your placement?" or, "Is your house straight?" or, "God first!"). Give every member of the family permission to ask anyone else how their spiritual walk is. Parents, don't be afraid to ask kids to pray for you, even if you don't give specifics. All you have to say is, "Mom just needs a little extra prayer today. God knows the details."

Encourage those who missed this week's On the Road Family Challenge to take advantage of each week's family learning experiences.

Discussion Questions

1. How did your On the Road Family Challenge go this week?
2. What are some specific ways your family can put God first?
3. What surprised you the most in this challenge?
4. What did you learn through this challenge?
5. How did you feel asking your children to help hold you accountable?
6. What are some ways children can be made to feel they contribute to keeping the family accountable to putting God first without driving the adults crazy?
7. Do you have anyone else in your life who you can be honest with who can ask you the tough questions and hold you accountable?
8. "These things I have spoken to you, so that in Me you may have peace. In the world you have tribulation, but take courage; I have overcome the world" (John 16:33 NASB). What are some challenges you face in putting God first in your life or your family's life?
9. "Therefore let him who thinks he stands take heed that he does not fall. No temptation has overtaken you but such as is common to man; and God is faithful, who will not allow you to be tempted beyond what you are able, but with the temptation will provide the way of escape also, so that you will be able to endure it" (1 Corinthians 10:12–13 NASB).

    What are some ways you can overcome these challenges in putting God first?

10. (If you have time) What are some ways we can teach our children to look at how they use their time and begin to take ownership of putting God first in their own lives?

Endnotes

Part 1

[1] God does not have a gender and, in fact, demonstrates male and female characteristics. God is also described in the Bible using both male and female metaphors (see, for example, the Father in Psalm 89:29 and Matthew 6:9, the midwife in Psalm 22:9–10, and the hen in Matthew 23:37). Hebrew (the original language of the Old Testament) does not have a gender-neutral pronoun, so it used the male. The majority of the metaphors for God are also male. In English, the neutral pronoun is reserved for inanimate objects, which God is most definitely not (see 2 Kings 1; Matthew 27:45–28:10; Revelation 19:11–21). Therefore, following tradition and in order to avoid confusion, the male pronoun will be used in this text.

[2] It used to be that all pronouns referring to God were capitalized as a reflection of His majesty, lordship, and superiority over us (see, for example, passages like Exodus 33:18–23; Isaiah 6:1–5; Colossians 1:15–20). There is a growing trend today to leave pronouns for God in lowercase, emphasizing instead His approachability (see passages like Hebrews 4:15–16). Still others leave the pronouns lowercase due to a lack of understanding or respect for who God truly is. I do not believe any of the sources I have quoted fall into the final category. I choose, however, to capitalize pronouns for God to remind myself that He is God Almighty and I am not, nor is anyone or anything else.

[3] When one comes across LORD in all capital letters, it stands for the name of God. When Lord and the name of God are used in conjunction, GOD in all capitals is used instead. Moses asks God His name in Exodus 3:13–15. "I AM WHO I AM" is the reply. "I AM" is the English translation for the Hebrew word *Yahweh*. In Jesus' day, the tradition was to say *Adoni* (translated "Lord") whenever one encountered the word "Yahweh" when reading a biblical text aloud. This was to keep from inadvertently taking the Lord's name in vain (Exodus 20:7). Much later, a compromise was made, combining the Hebrew consonants of Yahweh with the Hebrew vowels from Adonai in Jehovah. (Some purists find this combination more disrespectful than speaking the name Yahweh.) The important thing is to recognize the name of God and to use it with respect.

[4] Terry Gross, "Habits: How They Form and How to Break Them," *Author Interviews* (n.c.: npr books, March 5, 2012) (January 8, 2014). Available from *www.npr.org/2012/03/05/147192599/habits-how-they-form-and-how-to-break-them*.

[5] *The Interpreter's Bible*, vol. 8, ed. George Buttrick (Nashville: Abingdon, 1952), 265.

[6] Michael Yaconelli, *Dangerous Wonder* (Colorado Springs: NavPress Publishing Group, 1998), 15.

[7] If learners are not also doing *The Answer Book: A Devotional for Busy Families*, please be sure to include the "Bible Focus."

[8] This is a difficult concept for adults to grasp, let alone children. Nevertheless, it is what Scripture teaches, and it doesn't hurt to lay the groundwork early. Jesus is fully God and fully man. As fully

God, He always was and always will be. John 1:1 says, "In the beginning was the Word, and the Word was with God, and the Word was God." This refers to Jesus (see John 1:14–15). One of the things God does is give His Word, the Bible. "All Scripture is God-breathed and is useful for teaching, rebuking, correcting and training in righteousness, so that the servant of God may be thoroughly equipped for every good work" (2 Timothy 3:16–17, NIV). While Jesus is fully God, He is also fully human like you and me. How's that for a brain teaser? "For this reason he had to be made like them, fully human in every way, in order that he might become a merciful and faithful high priest in service to God, and that he might make atonement for the sins of the people. Because he himself suffered when he was tempted, he is able to help those who are being tempted" (Hebrews 2:17–18 NIV). Philippians 2:6–11 is a famous description of Jesus' two natures. When responding to kids' questions, try to keep it simple. Jesus is fully God and fully man. Before He was born as a baby, He was still God. That's when He spoke to the Old Testament writers as God.

[9] The "On the Road Family Challenge" is found in *The Answer Book: A Devotional for Busy Families*. These challenges may also be used apart from this devotional.

[10] John Babler, David Penley, and Mike Bizell, *Counseling by the Book* (Maitland, Fla.: Xulon Press, 2007), 44.

[11] More than one religion today teaches that human pain and suffering either purifies the soul or draws the attention of the divine (i.e., Roman Catholicism, Hinduism, Buddhism, and some Native American religions). Cutting (self-inflicted cuts for nonreligious reasons) is a similar idea, where a person either seeks to numb pain they cannot control with pain they think they can, or seek to call attention to themselves. The Bible teaches that God does not bring us evil; nor does He delight in it (James 1:13–14). He does, however, allow trials and pain in our lives as a result of sin (Genesis 3:17–19) to test and strengthen us (James 1:2–3; John 15:1–2; Job 1:8–12; 2:3–10). God Almighty is a loving God. He loves us as a Father loves His children (1 John 3:1). God always hears our prayers (Psalm 17:6), and He especially loves it when we come before Him with a heart that is truly sorry for our sins and humble before Him. The way to get the one true God's attention is to simply talk to Him. He knows everything anyway and is always watching and listening to us (Psalm 139). When answering kids' questions, be sure to emphasize God's loving care for us.

[12] Rick Warren, *The Purpose Driven Life* (Grand Rapids, Mich.: Zondervan, 2002), 70.

[13] Genesis 3:8 (NIV): "Then the man and his wife heard the sound of the LORD God as he was walking in the garden in the cool of the day ..."

[14] Mark Batterson, *In a Pit with a Lion on a Snowy Day* (Colorado Springs: Multnomah Books, 2006), 67.

[15] Dating Gideon's life and ministry with certainty is difficult. We know from 1 Samuel 8–10 that the tribal elders affirmed Saul as Israel's first king about 1020 BC; Thomas Brisco, *Holman Bible Atlas* (Nashville: Broadman & Holman Publishers, 1998), 97. Before Saul, God raised twelve judges in Israel to be military and spiritual leaders for the people, but God Himself was their king (1 Samuel 8:7–8). This was the system from the time Joshua led the people in to conquer Canaan after their wilderness wanderings with Moses. Scholars disagree on the dates for these judges, but all work backward from the date of Saul's coronation using biblical descriptions of the years each judge ruled. Matters are complicated, since some judges ministered at the same time in different parts of Israel. For more information, see the downloadable "Comparative Chronology Chart" available online at *kukis.org/Doctrines/Comparative_Chronology.pdf* (July 22, 2014), which compares the dates given in *Zondervan's Pictorial Encyclopedia of the Bible, vol. 3* (1976), 757; *The Reese Chronological Bible*, KJV translation, ed. Edward Reese (South Minneapolis, MN: Bethany House Publishers,

1980), 379–437; *The Narrated Bible in Chronological Order,* narrated by F. LaGard Smith (Eugene, Ore.: Harvest House Publishers, 1984), 347–385, 1693; and J. I. Packer, Merrill C. Tenney, and William White Jr., *The Bible Almanac* (Nashville: Thomas Nelson Publishers, 1980), 52–53.

16 Paul R. Kretzmann argues that the angel's greeting of "mighty warrior" was due to Gideon's qualifications—his physical strength, determination, and energy. *Popular Commentary of the Bible, Old Testament vol. 1* (St. Louis: Concordia Publishing House, 1923), 414. Gideon didn't see it, but later came to fulfill that calling.

17 C. S. Lewis, *Mere Christianity* (Westwood, N.J.: Barbour and Company, Inc., 1952), 45.

18 Bill Hybels and Mark Mittleberg, *Becoming a Contagious Christian* (Grand Rapids, Mich.: Zondervan Publishing House, 1994), 27.

19 Reggie Joiner, *Think Orange* (Colorado Springs: David C. Cook, 2009), 42.

Part 2

1 God does not have a gender and, in fact, demonstrates male and female characteristics. God is also described in the Bible using both male and female metaphors (see, for example, the Father in Psalm 89:29 and Matthew 6:9, the midwife in Psalm 22:9–10, and the hen in Matthew 23:37). Hebrew (the original language of the Old Testament) does not have a gender-neutral pronoun, so it used the male. The majority of the metaphors for God are also male. In English, the neutral pronoun is reserved for inanimate objects, which God is most definitely not (see 2 Kings 1; Matthew 27:45–28:10; Revelation 19:11–21). Therefore, following tradition and in order to avoid confusion, the male pronoun will be used in this text.

2 It used to be that all pronouns referring to God were capitalized as a reflection of His majesty, lordship, and superiority over us (see, for example, passages like Exodus 33:18–23; Isaiah 6:1–5; Colossians 1:15–20). There is a growing trend today to leave pronouns for God in lowercase, emphasizing instead His approachability (see passages like Hebrews 4:15–16). Still others leave the pronouns lowercase due to a lack of understanding or respect for who God truly is. I do not believe any of the sources I have quoted fall into the final category. I choose, however, to capitalize pronouns for God to remind myself that He is God Almighty and I am not, nor is anyone or anything else.

3 When one comes across LORD in all capital letters, it stands for the name of God. When Lord and the name of God are used in conjunction, GOD in all capitals is used instead. Moses asks God His name in Exodus 3:13–15. "I AM WHO I AM" is the reply. "I AM" is the English translation for the Hebrew word *Yahweh.* In Jesus' day, the tradition was to say *Adoni* (translated "Lord") whenever one encountered the word "Yahweh" when reading a biblical text aloud. This was to keep from inadvertently taking the Lord's name in vain (Exodus 20:7). Much later, a compromise was made, combining the Hebrew consonants of Yahweh with the Hebrew vowels from Adonai in Jehovah. (Some purists find this combination more disrespectful than speaking the name Yahweh.) The important thing is to recognize the name of God and to use it with respect.

4 Terry Gross, "Habits: How They Form and How to Break Them," *Author Interviews* (npr books, March 5, 2012) (January 8, 2014). Available from *www.npr.org/2012/03/05/147192599/habits-how-they-form-and-how-to-break-them.*

5 The "On the Road Family Challenge" is found in *The Answer Book: A Devotional for Busy Families.* These challenges may also be given the week before and used apart from this devotional.

[6] *The Interpreter's Bible*, vol. 8, ed. George Buttrick (Nashville: Abingdon, 1952), 265.

[7] Michael Yaconelli, *Dangerous Wonder* (Colorado Springs: NavPress Publishing Group, 1998), 15.

[8] "Absolute Truth," *Parenting* (Focus on the Family, 2000) (January 25, 2014). Available from *www. focusonthefamily.com/parenting/teen_booklets/absolute-truth.aspx.*

[9] John Babler, David Penley, and Mike Bizell, *Counseling by the Book* (Maitland, Fla.: Xulon Press, 2007), 44.

[10] According to Christian tradition, every one of the twelve disciples, except John, died for their faith. Peter was crucified upside down. Rev. Henry Alford, "Peter," *Bible Dictionary* (Nashville: Thomas Nelson Publishers, 1993), 504. Andrew was crucified. Rev. Edward Eddrup, "Andrew," *Bible Dictionary,* 40. James was put to death by Herod. Agrippa I. Eddrun, "James," 277. Attempts to boil John in oil failed, so he was sent to the labor mines before being exiled to the Isle of Patmos. Eddrun, "John, the apostle," 315. Legend says Philip was crucified upside-down. *The Apostle Philip (BiblePath.com)* (February 7, 2014). Available from *www.biblepath.com/philip.html.* Bartholomew was flayed alive and then crucified upside-down. Merrill F. Unger, "Bartholomew," *Unger's Bible Dictionary* (Chicago: Moody Press, 1976), 126. Thomas is said to have been killed by a lance. Unger, "Thomas," 1091. Legend says Matthew died a martyr in Ethiopia. Eddrun, "Matthew," 388. James the Lesser was thrown down from the temple by scribes and Pharisees. His body was then stoned and his head demolished with a fuller's club. (Just a hunch, but I think they were a little upset with the message he was preaching.) Eddrun, "James the Less," 277. Jude (also called Thaddeus and Lebbeus) may have been martyred in northern Persia. *The Apostle Jude (Thadaaeus) (BiblePath.com)* (February 7, 2014). Available from *www.biblepath.com/jude.html.* Simon the Zealot (also known as Simon the Canaanite) may have been martyred in Persia with Jude or in Lincolnshire, Britain. *The Apostle Simon (The Zealot) (BiblePath.com)* (February 7, 2014). Available from *www.biblepath.com/simon.html.*

[11] Peter W. Stoner, *Science Speaks* (Chicago: Moody Press, 1969), 109.

[12] Allowing enough time for the details of the Magi's visit to Herod (Matthew 2:1–12, 16, 19–20; compare verse 16 with Luke 2:16) and the dates Quirinius was governor of Syria (Luke 2:2), scholars determine Jesus was born in 7 or 6 BC. For a more in-depth discussion on dating Jesus' birth, see Robert H. Stein, *Jesus the Messiah* (Downers Grove, Ill.: InterVarsity Press, 1996), 51–60.

[13] *Bible Handbook* (Nashville: Thomas Nelson Publishers, 1993), 175.

[14] *Bible Handbook*, 195.

[15] Jesus began His roughly three-year public ministry (John 2:13; 6:4; 11:55) approximately AD 28, at thirty-three years of age (Luke 3:23). Pontius Pilate (Matthew 27:11–26) ruled in Judea through AD 36/37. Caiaphas (Matthew 26:57–68) reigned as high priest through AD 37. Jesus died on Friday (the day before the Sabbath), the 14th of the Jewish month of Nisan (Mark 15:42), as determined by the new moon. Looking back through the astrological calendar, this would be either AD 30 or 33. In order to fit Jesus' public ministry and the events that followed His resurrection, most scholars opt for AD 30. For a more-detailed discussion including the date of Jesus' life and death, see Stein, 51–60.

[16] Virginia Gorlinski, "Crucifixion," *Encyclopedia Britannica Online* (2014) (February 7, 2014). Available from *www.britannica.com/EBchecked/topic/144583/crucifixion.* Constantine the Great abolished crucifixion in the Roman Empire in AD 337.

[17] Rick Warren, *The Purpose Driven Life* (Grand Rapids, Mich.: Zondervan, 2002), 70.

18 *In a Pit with a Lion on a Snowy Day* (Colorado Springs: Multnomah Books, 2006), 67.

19 C. S. Lewis, *Mere Christianity* (Westwood, N.J.: Barbour and Company, Inc., 1952), 45.

20 The sun, moon, and several animals were worshipped as gods in Egypt, including crocodiles, fish, cows, cats, bulls, baboons, and jackals. Other gods were represented with animal heads and human bodies. "Egypt, Egyptian Religion," *Unger's Bible Dictionary*, ed. Merrill F. Unger (1966).

21 Circumcision is the removal of the foreskin of males. While today it is also done secularly for sanitation purposes, it was originated as a sign of God's covenant with Abraham (Genesis 17). When parents brought their child to the temple to be circumcised, they also brought the offering for the mother to be purified following childbirth (Leviticus 12).

22 See also Matthew 21:12–17 and Luke 19:45–46. Some scholars see these accounts as describing one cleansing of the temple at the end of Jesus' ministry rather than two, but there are issues with this view. One of these issues is the differences between John's account at the beginning of Jesus' ministry and those of the Synoptic Gospels' (Matthew, Mark, and Luke) recording of the cleansing of the temple the week of Jesus' crucifixion. One major difference is that Jesus fashioned a whip in John's account (John 2:15). Robert H. Stein, *Jesus the Messiah: A Survey of the Life of Christ* (Downers Grove, Ill.: InterVarsity Press, 1996), 186–187.

23 *Becoming a Contagious Christian* (Grand Rapids, Mich.: Zondervan Publishing House, 1994), 27.

24 To learn more about wicca, see Bill Gordon, "Wicca (Witchcraft)," *4Truth.net: World Religions* (North American Mission Board, 2013). Available from *www.4truth.net/fourtruthpbworld. aspx?pageid=8589952135.*

25 Craig S. Hawkins, *Witchcraft: Exploring the World of Wicca* (Grand Rapids, Mich.: Baker Books, 1996), 35.

26 *Think Orange* (Colorado Springs: David C. Cook, 2009), 42.